Effective Customer Care

Effective Customer Care

for Voluntary and Community Organisations

Amanda Knight

DIRECTORY OF SOCIAL CHANGE

Published by
The Directory of Social Change
24 Stephenson Way
London NW1 2DP
Tel: 0171 209 5151, fax: 0171 209 5049
e-mail: info@d-s-c.demon.co.uk
from whom further copies and a full publications list are available.

The Directory of Social Change is a Registered Charity no. 800517

First published 1999

ISBN 1 900360 36 5

British Library Cataloguing in Publication Data
A catalogue record for this book is available from the British Library

Designed by Kate Bass
Illustrated by Sonia Bellord
Edited and typeset by David McLean
Printed and bound by Antony Rowe

Other Directory of Social Change departments in London:
Courses and Conferences tel: 0171 209 4949
Charityfair/Charity Centre tel: 0171 209 1015
Research tel: 0171 209 4422
Finance and Administration tel: 0171 209 0902

Directory of Social Change Northern Office:
3rd Floor, Federation House, Hope Street, Liverpool L1 9BW
Courses and Conferences tel: 0151 708 0117
Research tel: 0151 708 0136

Contents

Foreword

Communication is vital to our business, and to society at large. At BT UK, we feel effective customer care is one of the key indicators of not only an organisation's overall efficiency, but also its commitment to all who use and provide its services. It is, therefore, a great pleasure to commend this lively and encouraging book, written specifically for voluntary and community organisations by someone who has wide experience of their needs.

Amanda Knight's definition of the complex term 'customer' rightly encompasses all stakeholders in a voluntary organisation, including clients, paid and volunteer staff, trustees and funders. Managing change on this scale and simultaneously keeping open the channels of communication takes time, effort, and commitment.

Good communication involves finding the time both to talk and to listen, not necessarily in that order. It is vital that all of us remember this most important of rules, from which so much else follows.

I wish every success to this book, and to those who use it to add value to the service they offer to others.

IAN A SMITH
Managing Director, BT UK Customer Service

ABOUT THE AUTHOR

Amanda Knight is the founding director of Carpenter Knight Associates and the Managing Director of The Telework Company. She has a BA in English and an MSc in Organisational Behaviour, both from London University. Her background spans the private, public and voluntary sectors. She specialises in personal development and consultancy in the fields of communication, marketing, public and media relations and the home/work balance.

She is passionate about customer care, seeing it as the missing ingredient in organisational success whether in the business or the voluntary sector. This book represents her personal and professional experience gained while working with business and charities to help them put customers first.

As well as writing for journals and magazines, Amanda is co-author of *Surviving Stress – a managers' guide* (FT Publications). She is a Trustee of The Whole Person Therapy Trust and a voluntary fundraiser with Hope and Homes for Children.

Amanda lives in Kent with her husband, Peter, and their small daughter, Zoë.

The Directory of Social Change wishes to thank British Telecommunications plc for its kind support of this publication.

Introduction

'Customer Care, it's just management jargon – it wouldn't work in our charity'
'It would be great to think about Customer Care but we just don't have the time'
'Oh no, not another initiative !'
'But we don't have customers in the Voluntary Sector'

These are just some of the reactions and comments I received when I first talked to people about this book. And perhaps they are right – what has an American way of doing business got to do with running a voluntary organisation? But giving good service and caring about customers is not just the seemingly superficial approach beloved of the fast food industry, it is a way of working that can benefit all organisations. There is far more to it than just being polite to people who walk through the door.

Many charities now find themselves operating in a competitive climate, tendering for work or competing for sponsorship; others are having to put more effort into raising funds from the public at large than formerly, and many more are reliant on generating income from products and services. These situations bring staff into contact with a wide range of customers or potential customers, and no organisation can afford to neglect the essential ingredient of successful business – satisfying customers' needs and making them feel special.

Some charities face a difficult challenge of working with service users or clients who would never regard themselves as customers, and who in the culture of the voluntary sector have perhaps never been treated as such. But just because your service is delivered for free doesn't mean that the recipients are not *customers*. Finding a customer service approach to satisfy both their needs and your organisational approach is not easy, which is why there is a section devoted to 'matching customer expectations' in Chapter Two.

This book is designed to help organisations in the voluntary or not-for-profit sector improve their relationships with users, clients, funders, supporters, staff, and volunteers – all of whom are a type of customer. If we can be better at managing their expectations then the scenario of an angry dissatisfied client berating the staff and storming out of the building should never occur, and if by chance it does then there are some techniques outlined in this book to help you handle that situation effectively.

In the following chapters there is information and advice on:

- what we mean by 'customer', direct and indirect;

- how to understand customer expectations and manage relationships;

- the relationship between image and customers;

- handling complaints and problems;

- dealing with staff and internal customers;

- using communication to improve customer care and a customer care checklist.

CHAPTER ONE

What is a Customer and What Do They Want?

What is in this chapter?
- a definition of what we mean by customers – paying and non-paying
- a discussion of the different types of customer
- a definition of what is meant by customer care

Imagine for a moment a different world: a world in which you never have to wait on a windy platform for a train that is running late – hoping in vain for someone to tell you what was causing the delay and when the train might actually turn up. A world in which it is not just common practice for someone to pack your shopping and carry it to the car, but that they do it willingly and with a smile. A world where every time you telephone a large organisation you are greeted by a human voice rather than a rendition of Greensleeves followed by a 'voicemail' message. A world in which you feel you only have to ask and the service, product or information you require appears without fuss, without delay and without aggravation.

A fantasy world perhaps; of course human error and delays do happen in the most efficient and customer-friendly organisations, but to understand what effective customer care really means you only have to think of the last time you were on the receiving end. Did you get the service you wanted? Did you feel that the people providing the service cared about whether you felt happy? Did you wish to complain but felt you couldn't because it would have been embarrassing, difficult, didn't seem fair because you hadn't paid for the service in the first place, would have meant a scene; or perhaps you felt it wouldn't have made any difference anyway?

WE ARE ALL CUSTOMERS
That is all very well, you may say, but there is a big difference between running a train service and running a charity. True, but the principle remains the same, and that is what makes customer care so straight-forward. We are all customers, we have all experienced both good and bad service – and we know which we prefer.

Putting the customer first

The Soggy Croissant Experience

Some time ago a colleague of mine persuaded me to go as her guest to a charity breakfast raising money for overseas aid. The keynote speaker was well known for his work in developing countries and had the reputation of being an entertaining and passionate speaker. The event was expensive, £25 (quite a lot for a breakfast), although she insisted that her company was paying for the tickets. It was terrible. The speaker was good but because of the way the tables were arranged we couldn't see him properly and the PA system meant it sounded as if he were speaking from inside a fish tank. In addition to that the breakfast was dire – lukewarm coffee and soggy croissants. However I suffered in silence – itching to complain but not wanting to embarrass my host. Oddly enough none of the other guests at the breakfast complained either, although we should have. After all we were all customers both of the charity hosting the event and of the hotel.

A CUSTOMER IS A CUSTOMER BY ANY OTHER NAME

Just because your customers don't walk in from the street, buy something and walk out with it in a plastic bag, that doesn't mean that you can ignore their needs or neglect their customer care. The important thing is not to get side-tracked in semantics. What you call them is irrelevant, it is how you treat them that matters – whether they have paid for your service or not.

All customers are equal

CUSTOMER CARE LAW 1: All customers are equal – regardless of whether they pay for your service or not

Here is a list of just some types of customer your organisation may have:

- Service Users
- Clients
- Purchasers
- Staff members
- Volunteers
- Trustees or management committee members

- Donors
- Supporters
- Sponsoring organisations
- Funders
- Local government
- National government
- Patrons
- The media
- Local community
- The general public
- Statutory bodies
- Other voluntary sector organisations

Throughout this book I will refer to all these types of customer as 'customers' for the sake of simplicity, although it may not always be the term most frequently used to describe them.

IDENTIFYING DIFFERENT CUSTOMERS

The list of 'customers' may seem long and unmanageable, each type requiring a special, individual, approach. However, customers can be broken down into two broad categories: **External** and **Internal**.

External customers in turn break down into two important subdivisions: *Direct* and *Indirect*. An *external direct* customer is someone who deals with your organisation on a one-to-one basis; they receive a service or product (whether they pay for it or not). An *external indirect* customer is one stage removed from your organisation. Their dealings with the organisation may be via another agency, or through a third party involvement. These customers are less well informed about you and their perception of your organisation is by definition coloured by someone else's interpretation. This means that you need to be much more aware of the customer care implications and work harder to ensure that these users receive good service and clear communication.

External direct customers are the largest and most diverse of your customer groups. External direct customers include all service users, whether or not they pay, clients and purchasers such as statutory authorities. The most likely to be neglected in terms of a customer care strategy are the non-paying service users, not because you do not deliver a good service, but because of the complex relationship between them and the organisation. These are the least likely group to make a complaint, their feelings towards the organisation may be ambivalent – a mixture of feeling grateful for your help but antagonistic because they would rather not have had to ask for it in the first place. They may be resentful but silent, and as such it is vital that your customer care policy takes account of this. (See Chapter Two on Meeting customer needs.)

Other external direct customers such as clients and purchasers may suffer the reverse, being those on whom most energy and attention is lavished because they are an important and influential source of income and support. But you should not assume that they are all looking for the same type of service. Purchasers, such as statutory authorities, are probably seeking a partnership based on knowledge and mutual understanding, whereas clients will want good effective service at a reasonable price whether they are one-off buyers or regular users.

External indirect customers are often influential and can be very important to the success of the organisation, but they are one step removed from the day-to-day running of the charity. Sponsors fall into this category – although they may know you well, their relationship is one step back from a purchaser of the service. But once you have got to know them they should then become an *external direct customer* and hopefully a repeat one. Naturally customer care is important when dealing with sponsors, but don't underestimate your importance to them, and make sure it is a relationship based on equality – not just gratitude for their funds. Most corporate sponsors actively welcome a partnership approach from the charities they fund.

Other external indirect customers include the media, politicians, local government officials, patrons, the local community and the wider public at large. Their perception of your organisation is based not necessarily on the gritty reality of life in the charity but on something they have read, seen or heard about you and your work. Ensuring that these customers receive the right image of you and are encouraged to act on your behalf is hard but rewarding work. Having these indirect customers on your side is an enormous marketing advantage.

Internal customers are by definition *direct* customers, because, although their contact with you may be infrequent, for example members attending an annual general meeting, their relationship is with the organisation directly, not via a third party or intermediary.

Internal customers include staff, volunteers, trustees and non-executive members of management committees. They know the organisation and are usually supportive and committed to its aims and objectives. However, they are often the most neglected customer group, taken for granted because they are supporters and they are not used to their full potential as advocates or

CUSTOMER CARE LAW 2: Customer care means not just meeting but exceeding your customers' expectations

champions of the organisation. These customers do not complain and if they do their complaints go unheard because they come from within. Ignore this group at your peril. They have the potential to be your biggest ally, but they can also be an influential and destructive critic if not handled with care and consideration.

WHAT DOES CUSTOMER CARE REALLY MEAN?

If there are three types of customer, does that mean there should be three approaches to customer care? The answer is No. Customers, whatever their relationship with you, are all seeking the same thing, a high quality service or product delivered in a friendly, efficient manner at a reasonable or appropriate cost.

Customer Care means ensuring that you deliver your stated service efficiently and effectively. It means meeting your deadlines and making the customer feel that it was not stressful for either of you. It means not whinging and complaining but working with a positive outlook and enjoying what you do, if you possibly can. It means behaving like a swan – gliding serenely along the surface of the lake without appearing to expend any effort, while paddling vigorously underneath.

A happy customer is one who leaves an encounter with your organisation saying 'That was an enjoyable, rewarding experience – I'll certainly work with them again'. Whatever the nature of your business, however difficult, uncertain or politically sensitive the area you work in, there is never an excuse for not putting the customer first.

This may sound demanding in our stressful world when computers fail and money runs out, when stress in the office means that staff are over-worked and things seem to go disastrously wrong, but if you follow the guidelines and work through the exercises in this book then you should be well on the road to getting your Customer Care right at least 50% of the time and that is a very good start. Of course 100% is your target but it pays to be realistic in the beginning.

CHAPTER TWO

Effective Relationship Management: Identifying and Meeting Customer Needs

What is in this chapter?
- how to identify customer needs
- the links between customer care and quality
- a customer care audit for your organisation
- a brief guide to 'relationship management'
- customer care for service users

MEETING CUSTOMER NEEDS

One of the main reasons why customer care sometimes fails is that people make assumptions about what customers do and do not want. In some cases, particularly with non-paying service users, customer care isn't even considered.

Case Study – Making assumptions doesn't pay

A small charity dedicated to working with disabled children was invited by a High Street bank's Trust Fund to apply for a research grant, although the bank did not specify what kind of research they were interested in. The charity leapt at the chance and the finance director and two trustees sat down with the Director and wrote a six-page application, full of facts and figures and cost benefit analysis of the efficiency of the organisation. They asked for £10,000 a year over two years to pay for a part-time research assistant who would conduct a detailed survey on the educational and social barriers facing disabled children and make recommendations for action by the local education authority and the schools in their region.

The Trust Fund turned down the application. The Director and trustees were upset and angry having been asked to apply in the first place and vowed never to waste their time and effort on making an application again.

This case study illustrates the danger of forgetting about the customer and their needs. In this situation there were three types of customer to be consulted. The first were the clients of the service – the children. What did they want and need from a research project? Shouldn't they have been involved in putting forward key areas of activity; after all they are on the receiving end of any deliberate or inadvertent discrimination, and they are the ones who overcome the obstacles. But, as with most charities, the finance director saw applying for funds as his job – after all he is the 'money man'.

CUSTOMER CARE LAW 3:
Never make assumptions about your customers

The second type of customer is the Trust Fund – why did the charity accept an unspecified request? Sometimes purchasers of our services do not know what they want. Never make assumptions for them. The charity should have asked them questions about the type of research, the target group, the purpose of any research project. Once the application was turned down they should have asked the bank why they invited the charity to tender in the first place.

The final type of customer is the hardest to question – the possible recipients of the research information. If the intention was to use information gathered to lobby the local authority and local schools, then the latter need to be consulted about their long-term strategies and policies – to ensure that any research is not wasted or worse still has not already been planned.

It seems hard to believe that a charity would make an application without having first asked those crucial questions but it does happen. It is just one example of many about assuming we know what the customer wants.

IDENTIFYING CUSTOMER NEEDS

Customers want to be listened to. Whether they are regular clients or one-time purchasers their opinions should shape your organisation's approach to marketing and product or service development. Some methods of consulting customers are outlined below – they are not all relevant all of the time but constantly gathering feedback and examining your activities in response is important.

CUSTOMER CARE LAW 4: Listen to your customers

Questionnaires

Questionnaires are the simplest and cheapest customer care feedback tool. They can be designed and produced in-house and can be tailored to a specific customer or product to ensure that you get direct feedback. What should a questionnaire look like?

A sample questionnaire is given in Appendix 1.

Rules for Questionnaires

1. **Keep it short and make it 'User Friendly'** – no one will fill in a six-page questionnaire for free; keep yours to a maximum of two A4 pages.

2. **Make it specific** – don't try to ask all customers about everything – stick to one product or service at a time.

3. **Customer relevance** – use a different questionnaire for different groups. If you need feedback from a particular group aim the questions directly at them.

4. **Vary the questions** – some can be 'closed' (*yes* or *no* answers only); some need options or tick boxes; others should encourage open-ended answers – such as 'tell us what you think works best about our drop-in service?' 'what is the worst aspect?'

5. **Encourage honesty** – don't lead customers to say only nice things about you. This is not a validation exercise and gathering feedback means there will be some answers you won't like!

6. **Offer an incentive to fill it in** – this could be a 'give away' or, if you are doing it face to face, a persuasive interviewer is sometimes enough.

Focus Groups

Beloved of political parties and market research organisations, the focus group is a very useful tool for refining customer care. These are small groups of individuals selected at random, through which you can explore and test ideas, perceptions or attitudes. By asking open-ended questions and collecting people's responses you can gather opinions directly from customers on how they feel about your organisation. To set up a Focus Group you need a facilitator who manages the process and ensures that people all get a chance to talk, a notetaker to capture all the comments, a neutral environment and a group of people picked at random. It is no good choosing your best customers who will just say positive things about you; if a Focus Group is to be worthwhile you must have a cross-section of customers from regular users, one-off users, those who have never used you and those who may use competitors. Focus Groups are open, unedited forums in which the facilitator asks an open question and encourages the participants to talk freely in response.

Guidelines for running Customer Focus Groups

Decide in advance the purpose of the Focus Group and choose your questions carefully – above all make them relevant.

Explain to the participants, before you start, the main purpose of the Focus Group and how you will use the information.

Stress the confidentiality of the exercise and do not attribute individual comments to a named person – even with their permission. This is not a 'collect a quote' exercise.

Choose a neutral, pleasant location. If you are asking people to give up time ensure that you have refreshments, that you have comfortable chairs and that there are no obvious barriers to conversation or distractions like noise.

Keep maximum numbers to 10 or 12 which allows everyone to talk and be heard. Ask open questions and give people time to respond. Don't be tempted to do all the talking 'to fill the silence'.

Break the group down into smaller groups to promote conversations and then ask them to report back their findings to the main group.

Record participants' remarks accurately word for word. If you censure, edit or summarise as you go along, you will filter the comments and the result will not be genuine feedback but your interpretation of what was said.

Sample focus group questions

- How do you think our organisation responds to requests for information?

- What is your impression of our staff?

- What words occur to you when you think about our organisation? (You could easily substitute 'organisation' with any of your key campaign themes – e.g., disabled children, orphans of war, etc.)

- What irritates or annoys you about our organisation, if anything?

- What aspects of our work particularly appeal?

- If you could change anything about us what would it/those things be?

Listening

Suggestion: if you are considering running a focus group, ask one of your corporate sponsors or contacts if they could help by providing a venue and one of their skilled human resources team to lead it for you. After all, as customers themselves, they have a vested interest in helping you make improvements.

Other ways to gather feedback

Other simple ways of gathering customer feedback include 'suggestion boxes' in your main reception or in shops; telephone surveys using an abbreviated questionnaire format (but beware of cold calling); examining the competition's successes – what works for them and why? Asking people face to face whenever they come into your office or while they are using the service is a good way of getting immediate feedback. Although it is not measurable in the sense of being part of a structured process it is an effective way of 'taking the temperature' of your customer service. Another route is to work with a complementary organisation, sharing a customer care survey either by distributing their questionnaire to your members and vice versa or by sharing the cost of a joint mailing.

> **CUSTOMER CARE LAW 5:** When you gather customer feedback, do something with it

There is absolutely no point in spending precious time and money finding out what the customers think if you then ignore the results.

WHAT HAS QUALITY GOT TO DO WITH IT?

If there is one piece of 1980s management jargon that makes people groan it is TQM – Total Quality Management. How many management initiatives have foundered on the rock of Total Quality and how much money has been wasted on elaborate TQM schemes, launched with a flourish, only to run out of steam months later without achieving their objective?

Why is TQM important in customer care?

The thinking behind the quality movement, which started in Japan after World War II, was that competitiveness depends upon customer satisfaction, which in turn is created through a combination of responses to customers' views and needs and the continuous improvement of products and services. The Japanese quality drive was inspired by an American called Edward Deming. It was not until the late 1970s that his American colleagues realised the value of what he had been saying for twenty years and by then Japanese manufacturers had established an almost unassailable lead in the production of everything from cars to computers.

Total Quality is a business philosophy that is founded on customer satisfaction, and is therefore about exceeding customer expectations, about going beyond those superficial 'have a nice day' stages to ensuring that customers' needs and desires are constantly met. As such it is an important part of any customer care programme. The two guiding principles that underpin the UK TQM movement are: a) careful design of the product – to eliminate faults during the design stage rather than trying to put them right at the end; b) ensuring that the organisation's systems are consistently capable of delivering that product or service. These two objectives can only be achieved if the whole organisation is working towards them, which is why it is called Total Quality Management.

What often went wrong with TQM since it became a well-known philosophy was that many organisations attempted to choose the parts they liked, rather than adopt a strategic approach. Quality Circles, groups of employees meeting on a voluntary basis to solve operational problems, were very popular in the 1980s. Many companies set them up but failed to act upon any of the results, so they just withered away.

What does achieving quality mean in terms of customer care? It means delivering a service or product without mistakes or faults; ensuring that the customer's needs are met fully and even exceeded; preventing any errors and causes for complaint and ensuring that the customer not only returns to re-purchase from you but tells others about their positive experience. A quality-focused organisation is also more likely to be one that reduces waste, cuts operating costs and gains high levels of repeat business.

One benefit of exceeding a customer's expectations is that it ensures a high level of loyalty. Naturally if you are unable to reproduce that level of service or product on a future occasion you will suffer from a double blow of heightened expectations and 'let down' so it is always better to give your best within the limits of your organisational capability. If that sounds like an excuse for not going 'the extra mile' as the American expression has it, it isn't. It is just advice to ensure that you keep consistent. Do not lower your expectations of your staff and their performance, but do ensure you can be consistent in delivering customer care.

CUSTOMER CARE LAW 6: Consistency counts in customer care

Positive thinking creates quality

One of my clients is a local welfare charity providing drop-in centres for the young unemployed. They only have four staff and operate two local centres in neighbouring towns, but they have been extraordinarily successful in attracting support and sponsorship. Local businesses give them help both in cash and in kind and the centre users are themselves active in helping to attract support. When I asked the secret of their success the Director said, 'Everyone who works here or comes to our centres is important. We believe in delivering quality and doing the best job we can everyday, despite the difficulties'. That kind of positive, focused thinking obviously makes a difference and it seems to pay off as the charity is currently raising money to move into bigger premises.

DOING A CUSTOMER CARE AUDIT

Do you know how customer friendly you are? Try this audit to assess your organisation's strengths and weaknesses and help you to build up a customer care action plan for future improvement. It is also a useful benchmarking tool for you to include in your evaluation process. (See Chapter Six on *Customer care policy* for more on benchmarking and evaluation.)

The Customer Care Audit

Q1 Who are our customers?

Ask every key member of staff, from the Chief Executive to the receptionists, shop workers, backroom staff, volunteers, and trustees and executive board members. Do they all list the same customers?

Q2 What is the value of each customer to the organisation?

Can those who answered Q1 say how much a regular or key customer is worth to the organisation in terms of revenue earned, sponsorship generated, or any measure of value (financial or non-financial) that is relevant to your organisation's core operation?

Q3 How many 'repeat customers' do we have?

Do you know? Does the marketing team know?

Q4 Do we have a customer care policy or statement?

Is it part of the organisational strategy or development plan?

Q5 Do we have a complaints procedure?

How often is it used?

Q6 Do we have a complaints follow-up process?

Is there a schedule for following up customers who have complained after a number of weeks/months? Do you use those complaints as levers for change in the organisation?

Q7 Do we update our database regularly?

At least once a month – to ensure good quality customer information, eg correct names/spellings, etc

Q8 Do we respond to simple enquiries within 24 hours?

Do you know whether the query was received by telephone, fax, e-mail or post?

Q9 Do we have customer care targets or targets for the number of customers we want to attract?
If so, are they published and well circulated? Are they monitored on a regular basis assessed through team briefings, etc?

Q10 Where are our priorities?
Are you going more for volume or for quality and how does that affect the delivery of your service/product?

Q11 What is our image amongst users/customers/other voluntary sector organisations?
If you do not know, conduct an image audit regularly – see Chapter Three.

Q12 Do we have a commitment to Quality?
Or is it 'cheap and cheerful will do'? How does that affect customer care?

Q13 Do we have a 'relationship management' strategy?
Is there a nominated person responsible for developing long term relationships with customers, users or purchasers?

Q14 How do we assess the needs of service users/non-paying customers?
Do you seek to involve the users when it comes to delivering the service? Are they silent recipients or active participants?

If the answer to any of the questions is 'No' then these are the areas that should form part of your action plan for creating better customer care. If the answer to all these questions is 'No' – *Don't panic.* If you work your way through the following chapters and exercises you will soon be able to change your answers from 'No' to 'Yes'.

THE SECRETS OF SUCCESSFUL RELATIONSHIP MANAGEMENT

Relationship Management is rather like TQM in that it is sometimes dismissed as a management 'buzzword' riven by cliché and used as an excuse for calling yet another meeting or carrying out one more organisational restructure. If, however, you can manage your customer relationships well you are far less likely to suffer numerous complaints, lost customers or alienated purchasers.

Relationship Management is an approach to building and maintaining open and effective communication between an organisation and its customers, whoever they may be. It involves developing an ongoing two-way conversation with those customers, a relationship rather than a one-off exchange; it means winning them, keeping them, and building loyalty through involvement. For organisations with wide ranging appeals and fund-raising campaigns, good 'relationship management' can mean thousands of pounds in donations; for others it may mean regular customers coming back to you for Christmas cards and gifts, and for others it can mean a statutory authority turning into a repeat purchaser choosing you as a service provider instead of the rival organisation down the road.

A brief guide to effective 'relationship management'

Be a smart communicator

Ensure you keep your customers informed about relevant activities or initiatives but do not overload them with information. Be smart in your communication by being selective. You can demonstrate that you understand their needs by giving them only the information they need and want.

Make it regular

This does not mean weekly mailings but it does mean setting regular dates for keeping customers informed (with newsletters, briefings events, etc) and then sticking to them.

Be flexible

If a customer wants a slightly different approach or service, try to be accommodating without over-stretching your own organisation. This could mean re-packaging information, services or products. If it does, see if you can get other customers interested so that it becomes cost effective.

Encourage and welcome their feedback

Well managed relationships thrive on two-way communication. Your customers have valid and useful things to say – use their comments and encourage them to contribute to increase your organisational effectiveness.

Be accurate

Keep accurate, regularly updated information on key customers, and make sure staff know about significant personnel changes. Nothing damages a relationship more than writing to the wrong person or addressing a mailing to someone who has left or, worse still, died.

Meet face to face

If at all possible try to get to know your regular customers and make sure they have some human contact either face to face or by telephone – don't just rely on mailings.

Involve them

Use some of the customer communication techniques described above, such as questionnaires or focus groups, to involve them and to seek their views on new developments or proposed projects.

Give good value for money

Some customers (particularly large ones) appreciate being offered a discount or something 'free' in addition to the service or product they have paid for. Don't be tempted to offer gimmicks but do allow room for negotiation and flexibility on price or services.

Be proactive

Go out and seek new customers and offer them an incentive to buy. Once you have made contact ask if they mind being kept informed of your organisation – don't just adopt the junk mail approach and put them on the database for ever more. Those that are really interested will be happy to receive your communications. If others do not want to know, save your organisation money by not contacting them.

Don't treat all customers the same

Remember the indirect customers such as the media, government or politicians, with whom the relationship is based on information exchange not on special offers and discounts. Don't neglect them and don't take them for granted.

CUSTOMER CARE FOR PEOPLE WHO DON'T LOOK LIKE CUSTOMERS

Those of you whose customers do not fall into the direct money in/service out category may have read the chapter so far and thought 'none of that applies to us'. But it does, because we need to achieve a customer conscious culture – that is an environment which always considers the needs of its customers by looking at the world from their point of view. For example, if your charity delivered home-based care to the elderly and housebound, when it came to 'thinking customer' they would be your starting point. How do you ensure that you understand their requirements and exceed their expectations? I believe that this approach is applicable in all contexts although the language and some parts of the process might vary.

Here are some ideas and thoughts on creating a customer culture for service users:

- ask for their views – seek honesty, not compliments;

- involve them in planning and delivering new services;

- take purchasers, sponsors and influencers out to meet users face to face, so they see what the issues and problems are;

- never make assumptions about what they want or need;

- encourage suggestions and feedback on a regular basis. For instance, you might set up a user feedback group, made up of volunteers, who can help keep communication open between you (the provider) and them (the users);

- delegate decisions to front-line staff who work with the service users;

- remember people live up to or down to our expectations of them – expect more and you should receive more;

- don't always assume that people cannot or do not want to pay. For some charities giving people the chance to make a small voluntary contribution, even if it is only 50p, means the user/supplier relationship shifts so that customer care becomes much easier to implement (obviously there are always some people who need help and do not have resources available, so this isn't a hard-and-fast rule);

- don't be discouraged if they do not want to be involved – keep trying.

CHAPTER THREE

The Importance of Image

What is in this chapter?
- what image means in customer care
- what creates your image and ways to improve it
- creating a customer care culture

IMAGE MATTERS

We live in an image-conscious world: people judge on appearances and make decisions based on fleeting impressions of events or organisations. Think of one of the most famous images of the late 1990s – the photograph of Diana, Princess of Wales, walking across a landmine site dressed in mask and flak jacket. The work of the landmine charity did not begin on the day she did her walk, nor did its mission or operations change as the result of her involvement. Yet that one powerful image did more to unlock donations than any other single thing the organisation did.

And on the subject of images associated with the Princess, think of the reaction to the decision by the Diana, Princess of Wales, Memorial Fund to pay for professional services rendered by a firm of solicitors dealing with the hugely complicated area of copyright and intellectual property law. The negative reaction of the public was extreme, exacerbated by the fact the fund had at that point still not contributed to a single charity project.

People's perceptions are tremendously powerful and cannot be controlled. The image your customers have of your organisation could be based on something as fickle as their reaction to a photograph or an item of television news.

> **CUSTOMER CARE LAW 7:** Image is based on perception and you cannot control perceptions – only influence them

> **Image influences**
> A friend of mine was listening to the radio one day and heard an interview with the Director of Womankind, a charity working in the developing world to set up local projects which allow women to become self-sufficient and earn a small income for themselves and their families. She was so impressed by what she heard that she immediately set up a generous annual standing order for a donation although before that day she had never heard of the charity.

WHAT CREATES THE IMAGE OUR CUSTOMERS HAVE?

The image your customers have is vital to your success in creating and maintaining high levels of customer care. So what affects it and how can you influence it?

Your customers will gain an image of your organisation through:

- your staff – including volunteers
- your external communications
- your publications
- your office and reception
- your advertising
- your outlets – including shops, advice bureaux, regional offices
- your trustees/executive committee and patrons
- your news coverage/public relations

Let's look at each of these in turn:

Staff

Staff are the most important weapon in the 'Image Wars'. How your staff anticipate and respond to customer requests, whoever the customer and whatever the request, sets the tone for the relationship. How well would your staff do in the Image Audit below? Do you feel confident that they represent the best aspect of your organisation or is there room for improvement?

Volunteers are sometimes difficult to categorise when thinking about customer care. Some of your volunteers may also themselves be users, so they fall into more than one category being at times both internal and external customers. When they are working with you directly they should be treated the same as staff, which means they need to adhere to the same standards that you expect from staff, and be subject to the same disciplines in relation to good service. However, as they also have an outsider's perspective of the organisation, make use of this when considering your image. Ask your volunteers how they see the organisation, what their friends and acquaintances think of it and where they feel there is room for improvement. Use the Image Audit for them as well as for staff.

Image Audit: Staff

- Do they listen to customers before offering suggestions, advice, products or services, or do they leap in with a range of selling techniques?

- Do customers get a chance to explore the options, whether buying a 20p book from your charity shop or committing £5,000 of local authority money on housing services?

- Do your staff understand the importance of body language and non-verbal signals, especially when talking to customers on the telephone (see Chapter Four)?

- Are they friendly and professional or cool and distant? Worse still, are they too friendly – is yours an immediate first name culture? In some situations that's fine, but it is not always relevant or appropriate, and can make customers feel uncomfortable.

- Do they adopt an 'all customers are equal but some are more equal than others' approach? Treating the important clients with servility and ignoring the rest?

- Do they understand the value of every customer and make time to empathise with them?

> **Suggestion:** Avoid the high street bank approach – whenever you call you hear 'Hello, thank you for calling XYZ bank, my name is Sandra, how can I help you?'; You get the sense that someone is reading a script. It is much better to say simply 'Good morning, ABC Charity' and let the customer lead, adding 'How can I help?' only if it is a sincere, natural offer.

External communications

Your staff may be doing fine, but are they working with their feet stuck in treacle? What is the prevailing organisational culture. Is it one which allows them the freedom to answer questions efficiently, to exercise their intelligence and let their expertise show? Does a Customer Care Culture exist in your organisation or do some of your staff regard the public as a nuisance who clog up the efficiency of the office? What are standards of performance like for vital external communications such as answering the telephone? Remember the time when the telephone was answered by a human voice not a jingle? Don't let your office adopt the 'never answered telephone' syndrome.

CUSTOMER CARE LAW 8: Always answer the telephone within 4 rings – you never know who is on the other end of the line

It is not just the time taken to answer telephones, it's what happens next that counts. Even if your staff are friendly and professional they can be hampered by not having the correct information to answer questions from the public. Organisations often put front-line personnel who do not know enough onto the telephone which means that every call has to be referred, or worse still put on hold, while the overworked information office tries to deal with a hundred questions at once.

Suggestion: give the switchboard and front-line personnel basic knowledge and information on your services or products so they can field questions themselves and thereby save time and improve customer service.

If messages are taken, how long does it take to call back? All customer queries should be dealt with within 24 hours. (In a TQM environment even that would be too long. The norm is that infamous 'zero carried forward' which means nothing left from today gets carried over into tomorrow – but that is not always realistic.) If 24 hours is not attainable then leave it no longer than 48 hours. It is reasonable to respond 'I got your message – I am dealing with it and I will have an answer for you by tomorrow'. Customers want to be kept informed and that means telling them what's happening – even if it's 'I don't know but I know a person who does....'.

The 24-hour rule should apply to in-coming mail as well, but a 48-hour turn-around is acceptable for simple postal enquiries. Don't be tempted to simply reply 'thank you for your letter, we are dealing with the matter' and then file it in the pending tray for six weeks. Find out the answer and deal with the enquiry immediately if at all possible. The secret of good time management is to handle paper once only. Holding letters in pending trays takes time – it doesn't save it.

THE CUSTOMER-FRIENDLY ANSWERPHONE

It is not always possible to answer every call in person, so make use of the technology available to make the answering service really helpful and friendly. If you have a voicemail system encourage everyone in the office to leave a similar message, not so that your staff sound like robots but to ensure that customers receive a consistent positive image. An example might be: 'Hello, this is Jane in the Finance Department; sorry I am unable to take your call, please leave your name and message after the tone and I will call you back as quickly as possible. If your message is urgent, please call my colleague Sam on extension 425. Thank you'.

For out-of-hours calls or call-waiting systems where a caller hears a recorded voice rather than a human one, make sure that you provide all the necessary information so that they know when to call back, or know how long they will be waiting on line. Set a standard for replying to answerphone messages – within the same day if possible or on the following morning.

Publications

Publications say a great deal about your organisation and your approach to customers. The prevailing climate amongst the voluntary sector is still one which frowns on the idea of spending money on non-essential items such as publications, stationery and other printed material, with the result that they are often produced on a low budget, leading to poor design, low quality and unprofessional results. While no one is advocating an advertising agency approach of high gloss and high expense, your customers deserve a well designed, well produced newsletter that looks as if time, thought and expertise has gone into it, even if it is printed on cheap paper. Value your customers, treat them with the respect they deserve and do not let the 'this is the voluntary sector – we don't spend money on that' attitude be an excuse for low-grade publications.

It is not only the look of publications and printed items that matters but also the quality of the writing and the accuracy of the content. Spend time, and if necessary money, on getting it right, avoiding mistakes and typographical errors. Ensue you have well written articles, illustrated by interesting and relevant photographs or illustrations: there are many freelance writers available who, for quite small fees, can produce a well written piece which is a joy to read.

Corporate image and logos

Businesses spend huge sums of money on their corporate image; many of them employ costly agencies to design obscure, complex logos that only the 'creative' team understand. If you are thinking of having a new logo, then follow these simple guidelines:

Test it out on people who know nothing about your organisation. Ask you friends and relations or total strangers.

Try it out on some existing customers. Ask them what they think the logo represents: you might be amazed at what they say.

Make sure it reproduces as well in black-and-white on photocopiers and that it can be enlarged for posters or reduced for business cards and still look good.

Avoid arty, 'creative' or obscure designs – simple, clean, clear images work best.

Don't be tempted by an expensive design agency – try the local art school or sixth form college students first (redesigning your logo could be an art project, welcomed by students and teaching staff because it is 'real').

The £1,000 logo

A new charity, set up to run a UK-wide campaign, commissioned a London agency to produce a corporate style and logo for them. The end-product, while very arty, was in red white and blue (not popular in Scotland or Northern Ireland) and didn't photocopy well – coming out a strange shade of grey. By the time all this was discovered, letterhead and business cards had already been printed and, despite a bill over £1,000 from the agency, the charity ended up redesigning the logo themselves (with the help of a friendly printer) and throwing away thousands of sheets of unusable paper.

Office and reception

For some of your customers the first point of contact is not the telephone but your reception area. How does it score on the Image Audit?

Image Audit: Reception

- What does your reception area look like?

- Is it open, clean, light, and welcoming?

- Are there comfortable chairs to sit on?

- Is information about the organisation readily available with examples of your work and your successes displayed confidently?

- Do you have a press cuttings book for people to look through while they wait?

- Where are the reception staff? Are they glued to the telephone trying to double up as telephonists?

- Do people get acknowledged as they walk in or do they have to go up to the desk before anyone takes any notice of them?

> **CUSTOMER CARE LAW 9:** Your welcome must be
> professional and friendly while your service is immediate and effective

Can you say that the welcome is professional and friendly and that you deliver effective service? If not, look at the questions above and see how you could change your reception area to make it more attractive to customers and visitors. Of course, there is little you can do about the location, but, providing you have a welcoming approach inside the building, the outside is largely irrelevant. A charity I visited recently had its offices in an old primary school hut in the middle of a disused playground, a rather gloomy prospect on the outside. Inside, however, the office was alive with activity, full of useful information leaflets and staffed by a welcoming receptionist who already knew I was expected that day.

> **Suggestion:** if you know you have visitors coming, give your receptionists their names in advance so they can be greeted warmly and welcomed, just as you would someone in your own home.

The Telephone Vs Reception Debate
A housing and homeless charity was so short-staffed it had to double up the switchboard operator and the receptionist. However, as they had a standard of performance that meant telephones had to be answered within 4 rings, even if the receptionist was deep in conversation with a client she had to interrupt to answer the telephone, leaving the person standing at the desk, ignored. In the end the receptionist decided to adopt a 'take a message' campaign. If she was dealing face to face with a client and the telephone rang she would politely say 'Excuse me, may I just answer this and take a message' then answer the telephone saying 'Could I please take your number and call you back in ten minutes. I have a client with me at present'. It didn't always work because sometimes the caller became insistent or she had to put calls through to other parts of the building, but on the whole it helped reduce the stress and conflicting demands on her time.

Advertising and promotion

The image you project through advertisements and promotional literature will be fundamental to how many of your customers see you. Your image must be consistent with your main activities and message. People need to be able to identify your organisation instantly. Our world is dominated by highly sophisticated advertising material with many subtleties and hidden messages, or overly clever adverts for obscure products. Don't be tempted down that route: make your message clear and consistent. Always remember to include your logo and don't try to reach too many audiences at once. Once you have decided on the type and style of advertising approach then beware that you may become branded with that image alone. If so, when you want to try a different approach, it will be almost impossible.

Greenpeace – image builders at work

What images does one get from the newspaper adverts Greenpeace places – pictures of tiny inflatables dwarfed by huge oil tankers or whaling ships? Dramatic, fast moving, daring – an organisation that isn't afraid of taking on the big boys. Those pictures stay in the mind and are vastly reinforced by Greenpeace's clever use of media images and technology. They not only take extraordinary pictures of their people landing on the oil platform, they then ensure the world's press received those pictures on their desks via the Internet in time for the day's papers. As a result the general public has them firmly fixed in their mind as eco-warriors.

Advertising is not the medium for building long-term customer relationships. It is the one hit, fundraising, profile raising technique. Do not view it as a way of keeping customers; it is better designed for gaining new ones or raising funds associated with particular events or campaigns. It can be a useful information tool for spreading key messages but as it is an indirect medium you cannot be sure all your customers will have seen it. If you have something important to say to them do so direct through a mailshot or newsletter.

Outlets

Outlets include shops, drop-in centres, advice bureaux, and regional offices. All these public spaces are a vital part of creating the right customer environment – right for your customers and right for your charity. They do not have to look like Harrods but they must be enticing. With over four or five charity shops in every high street yours must stand out. Cleanliness, themed window displays, the latest items in stock all help to attract customers in. Once people are inside, the layout of the space is also important. Is it easy to move around and are things visible, or is every shelf and bit of floorspace crammed with stock?

What happens then? Are the staff encouraging but not pushy? Are they able to spot when a customer might need help without doing a hard sell? For some people the joy of charity shopping is browsing, but others may be looking for something special and would welcome some help.

As far as drop-in centres or advice bureaux are concerned, the overall impression must be one of a non-threatening welcome, with as few barriers as possible to prospective clients. Sitting behind a desk gives the staff member a sense of security, but it immediately distances them from the person who has come in to seek help (see Chapter Five for ideas on body language and welcoming gestures) and they may have had to pluck up their courage for days before walking through your door. Remember, if you offer a listening and respectful ear, you will break down the fears and create a safe space for people to communicate.

'Outreach' services should be included under this heading, because, although they do not have a centre or a building, the customer relationship is paramount when one is delivering a service directly into someone's home, (as care assistants do), or in someone else's environment (as a hospice visiting service does). Staff and volunteers who work in this area are highly skilled, sympathetic and in-tune with the needs of their clients. They may feel that customer care is irrelevant because their whole job is about caring for people. However, one must not take their talents for granted – as internal customers the staff need support and recognition and the external customers who receive such services have an important role in giving feedback about how the service works, the benefits and possible improvements. These types of outreach activities need special and sensitive handling and should be included in any customer care policy you have.

Trustees, executive committee and patrons

These people are a tough group to work with, but a vital part of your image lies in their hands. Are your trustees customer conscious? Do they embody a customer care culture, or are they bogged down in the minutiae of accounts, committees and minutes? What kind of image do they present to the outside world when they go about their daily lives – are they likely to talk with enthusiasm about your organisation, praise the staff and sell a positive and enticing message to their audience, or are they prone to grumbling and complaining about the late arrival of expenses? If appropriate, encourage one of your trustees or management board to become a customer care champion – someone who will be on your side in trying to change the organisational culture and who will keep the complex customer picture in sharp focus when it comes to decision-making in meetings. A simple 'but what about our customers?' question asked at the right moment can make a difference.

Patrons can carry even more weight than trustees but only if they are active on your behalf. Are they aware of their impact on potential customers and how their image affects your charity? As a discreet marketing tool an active patron can unlock much support and interest for your organisation which in turn attracts customers. Success breeds success, so make sure that you use your patron effectively by getting them to promote your cause in whatever way they can.

News coverage and public relations

These are the hardest of all image-making activities to control or even to influence. Yet they are the most powerful in many people's minds. You can at least ensure that your message is consistent. For example, if you work with children, never send out a news release or give a press briefing without having a child's point of view to share with the journalist. Demonstrate to the outside world that your customers come first. Even if your message is distorted in reporting, some of the customer focus will come through.

Thinking customer

Remember that potential customers will judge you on your public profile, so do not court publicity for its own sake. Target what you want to say and to whom. Use your media and PR strategies to complement your customer care strategy. In customer care terms the cliché 'there is no such thing as bad publicity' is completely wrong . Negative publicity sticks in people's minds far longer than positive publicity.

THE CUSTOMER CARE CULTURE

You need to adopt a new approach if you are to turn the organisational culture from reactive customer-tolerant to proactive customer-friendly. Consider a few of the following ideas:

Think *Customer* – try to generate a sense of excitement and energy amongst your staff about the concept of customers. Everyone needs to see that they are responsible for customer communication. Allow individual departments and teams to explore their own notions of what a customer is and what this means to them. They may prefer another term like client or purchaser or user – that is fine because it is the attitude you are after, not the actual name.

Value the customer – persuade everyone to think about how much each customer is worth, not just financially but in terms of what they bring to the organisation. As with the naming of customers, clients, etc, encourage acceptance of the idea at all levels in the organisation. If the finance director wants to put a £ next to each customer – fine. The marketing team may value customers in terms of how they fit into their marketing strategy, which key target groups they represent, which areas they come from, etc. The important thing is to make everyone see that every customer counts.

Remember that *everyone* **is a customer** – it is not just those who pay who matter. The secret of customer care is to treat every customer with respect, and aim to deliver the highest standard of care and service that you can.

Train your team in customer service – share with them your customer care plans and policy and get them to add ideas and suggestions. Try not to allow a gloss of superficial customer care to get in the way of giving good service that represents value for money.

Set targets – if you have a strategy you must have targets so that you can monitor progress. Make these realistic and achievable but challenging enough to motivate the front-line team.

Have Customer Forums – so that the backroom team, who may not deal direct with customers on a daily basis, get to see who the organisation is working with, why they are important, and what they mean to the success of your charity.

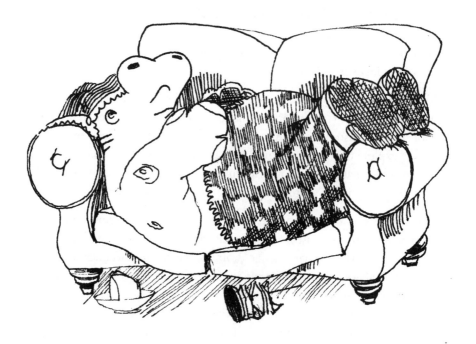

The Idle Hippo

CHAPTER FOUR

Identifying and Overcoming the Barriers to Customer Care

What is in this chapter?
- what stops us delivering customer care: barriers and problems
- changing the internal culture
- internal customers – who are they and why do they matter
- managing time and planning
- different types of customers

WHAT STOPS US DELIVERING CUSTOMER CARE?

There are several natural barriers in any organisation to making customer care a reality, some easier to tackle than others. Acknowledging that they are there is an important first step to implementing a more responsive customer-focused culture.

Some of the barriers are to do with organisational culture and the effect it has on people who work for you; others may be related to the physical limitations of resources, be they time, money, or equipment. The nature of your product or service could make customer care difficult; and at times the customers themselves seem to be the cause of the problem.

WHAT CREATES ORGANISATIONAL CULTURE?

Organisational culture is an amorphous object, a collection of attitudes and moods which permeate the organisation, affecting the staff and being fed by the staff in turn. This cycle has to be broken if you are hoping to make a cultural shift and you must start at the top. Senior managers set the tone when it comes to cultural change. If they demonstrate commitment then other staff will follow more readily. Without top-level commitment you are powerless to create real change. An action plan follows later in this section for tackling staff attitudes as a lever to culture change.

External perceptions of your organisation reinforce its culture as well. The traditional culture within the voluntary sector has not been one of high customer service; many organisations do not perceive themselves as having customers at all – they think only in terms of members, supporters, clients or users. The organisational philosophy that you exist 'to provide a much-needed service at low cost to those whom society neglects' combines with the historical precedents of 'working very hard for small returns'.

The notion of 'Voluntary' in the voluntary sector looms large, often placing unrealistic expectations upon staff about how hard they should work, how little they should be paid and how small a budget the organisation can survive on. Constantly overworking and under-resourcing creates an unsettled atmosphere and therefore attempting any new policy or procedure can be difficult. If the prevailing way of working is 'firefighting' – a reactive crisis-managing environment rather than a calm, planned and proactive one – then the pressure and the stress levels will be high.

Undoubtedly many charities or non-profit organisations are underfunded. Often the pressure is a result of poor time management and cultural habit. Initiating a customer care policy could be just the right vehicle for changing that culture and introducing new working habits which in turn relieve organisational stress.

These cultural norms are fed by staff behaviour and attitudes. Some staff create stress in the office through poor planning and weak time management. Others do not want change, having a strong sense of identity with the existing culture, firmly believing that they are right. Some others want to make changes but find themselves 'lone voices in the wilderness' and give up in despair. Often internal preoccupations get in the way of seeing the wider vision of why we are here and what we are doing. Couple these with the natural resistance found in all organisations and you have a difficult situation to deal with.

How can you shift to make customer care a dominant feature of your operating culture? Remember that if it is to work then it must be a shared vision, not just an optional extra that staff do when they feel like it. The place to start is with staff attitudes. Change these and you can reorganise ways of working and initiate procedures which support a customer friendly environment in no time.

The Customer Care Menagerie

Some organisations face an internal 'zoo' of attitudes that get in the way of delivering quality customer care. The animals most commonly found in organisational menageries are:

The Idle Hippo – this kind of person is prone to lolling around while others rush about caring for customers. They are inclined to consider any kind of customer communication as far too much effort and are unlikely to hear comments from unhappy customers due to the extremely small size of their ears.

The Slithery Snake – while smooth and charming to a customer's face the Snake hisses behind their back; difficult to pin down and tackle on poor customer care because their speed in slithering away from difficult situations when the going gets tough.

The Eager Monkey – while scoring '10 out of 10' for enthusiasm the Monkey usually goes too far making promises it cannot keep leaping about chattering with excitement and totally missing the subtlety of the customer's request. Groups of monkeys together can be disastrous because they distract each other from the job in hand, telling jokes, hanging around in groups, socialising and swapping stories.

The Elephant Never Forgets... that a long time ago someone in management mentioned customer care, set up an initiative and it didn't work – so what's the point of trying again!

The Ostrich with its Head in the Sand – customer! ... what customer?

The Aloof Leopard – leopards are above the niceties of customer care. After all the very fact that the organisation exists is reason enough, so who needs customers? When they do deign to deal with customers directly the effect is so unnerving for all concerned that everyone does their best to keep the Leopard and customers far apart.

The Timid Rabbit – is quite happy to deal with customers, except that customers are so demanding and are inclined to bully the poor rabbit into a state of complete paralysis. Rabbits prefer to view customers from a safe distance where they can make a quick exit if needs be.

The Frantic Squirrel – with so much internal organisation to be managed and so many files to be processed, there really isn't time for customers. The organisation cannot function without adminis- tration, and customers just get in the way.

CHANGING STAFF ATTITUDES

Before you think about change you must decide where the problems lie. Do any of the following statements reflect the attitude of your staff?

- 'Customers – that's too commercial for us'

- 'Our users do not want to be thought of as customers'

- '...they don't pay'

- 'We are a charity and we provide a service – we aren't a supermarket'

- 'It wouldn't make any difference what they (the customers) say, we couldn't change what we do'

- 'We can't afford that kind of luxury'

- 'I haven't got the time – I'm too busy running the office'

- 'It's hard enough just doing the job now – the last thing I need is another bloody policy'

If you have already done an image audit on your staff (see Chapter Three) this should have highlighted some of the habits prevalent in the organisation. With this and a sense of your staff's attitudes you are now in a strong position to introduce different ways of working.

An action plan for shifting staff attitudes

1. Start from where they are: encourage your staff to be open about their attitudes and try to get possible barriers out in the open so you can deal with them one by one. Set up a focus group or special team meeting to discuss customer issues; don't just tack it onto an already overcrowded agenda of an existing meeting.

2. Understand what causes their attitudes: what preconceptions do the staff have which might influence their view of existing users? Are they based on stereotypes which are caused by age, race, gender, class or tradition? If your service users have always been viewed as recipients of charity rather than as customers then you have some organisational rethinking to do.

3. Listen to what the staff say: try not to dismiss their views as being 'old fashioned' or stereotyped. Seek their ideas on how to deal with customers and try to encourage 'ownership' of any customer care initiatives that you are planning. This may mean appointing a well respected member of staff as Customer Champion, someone who will try to win over doubters; or you could allocate specific tasks to the sceptics to let them see for themselves the value of good customer relations. Putting the chief executive on the switchboard for a couple of hours is an excellent way to change their view about the general public!

4. Set targets and ensure that you have a monitoring procedure in place: when you instigate a new way of customer friendly working you need to check on progress. Targets can be numerical – ie. increase users by 10% over the next 12 months, or quality-related – how much time each enquiry takes and how you encourage and use feedback from customers. The benefit of targets is that they allow to you shape your policy in response to customer behaviours. The downside, however, is that some staff may view the idea of targets as unnecessary management control or, worse still, the 'big brother' approach.

5. Find a champion: preferably someone with organisational clout who will spread the positive message that all customers count.

6. Ensure top level commitment: you need to have the chief executive and senior managers on your side *before* embarking on culture change. Staff attitudes will not change unless they see real evidence of leadership and commitment from the top.

7. Take your time: don't be too ambitious and try to rush things. Set sensible targets for changing the culture and remember that habits are hard to break. It can take some people a long time to change their approach.

8. Don't be afraid: of making mistakes or of upsetting people. If you are committed to customer care as a philosophy and you have senior support then you will manage to shift the culture eventually; but inevitably you will upset some people somewhere along the line. Listen to their opinions, try to encourage them to see your point of view, but don't let them put you off or bully you into backing down.

9. Involve the volunteers: although not on the payroll and perhaps only working one day a week, volunteers are as important as staff when it comes to perpetuating an organisational culture. Ensure all volunteers are kept fully informed of plans, and encourage their contribution and active participation in the change process. They are often dealing directly with customers and they can be instrumental in helping you develop customer care if they are fully involved.

Suggestion: examples of successful organisations which have done similar exercises will help to convince people that adopting a new approach is worthwhile. Try to find a charity where customer care is working well and use them as a model of best practice, both to provide some benchmarks for your own organisation and to help you to demonstrate the benefits and win over the sceptics you may have.

THE INTERNAL CUSTOMER – WHO ARE THEY AND WHY DO THEY MATTER?

If you wish to shift staff attitudes to ensure a friendly approach to the outside world, you may also need to shift your own perception about internal customers. If your organisation has never thought of staff, volunteers, trustees, non-executive management teams or patrons as being types of customer you will need to remind managers that they are equally important to external ones. Without the energy and skills of internal customers you would not succeed, but how many of us are inclined to take their commitment and hard work for granted?

The pressures of getting the job done on time sometimes result in our failing to support and reward the very people who meet that target. Good internal customer care should be part of your ongoing management strategy, a key element in your staff development plans and as consistent and high quality as you can possibly manage.

I am not suggesting that you have separate accountability for every individual task. In many small organisations this can generate more bureaucracy and administration without increasing productivity. But by viewing staff as having the same rights and expectations as your external customer you will be generating a culture which encourages good customer care, and in which it is the norm rather than the exception in terms of behaviour and attitudes.

How to create an internal customer culture that supports your staff

Try to view all staff, volunteers, and other internal customers as having shared needs for information, support and operational resources in addition to having specific requirements based on their relationship with your organisation. A trustee, for example, might need short bursts of intensive attention when they are working a particular project or heading an internal action team for you, followed by periods in which they are not involved as much and just need to be kept up to date.

Thinking of staff as customers is complicated because they are both providers and users. If they are the service or the organisation's 'product', how can they be its customers? What is needed is an approach which recognises the service and communication needs of staff and which values them as highly as external customers without attempting to generate an artificial culture. As well as making sure you have excellent communication internally, you can adopt some of the initiatives outlined here.

Team briefings

First developed as a way of cascading information down through large companies quickly, a process known as Team Briefing can be adapted into an effective method of keeping all staff involved, even if they are working in different offices at different times. Team Briefing is not meant to be a consultation discussion process, but an information sharing tool to ensure that all your team are kept up to date with information. Whether fortnightly or monthly, each meeting will be short and restricted to telling staff all they need to know about organisational issues such as finance, projects, new developments, staff changes etc. Managers and team leaders should support team briefings with more open consultative meetings in which staff feel able to share their responses or issues with one another.

Remember that one of the cornerstones of customer care is keeping all customers informed and involved, and regular opportunities for two-way staff communications have to be built into your organisational schedule. It is no good hoping that they will happen by accident or because you all happen to be in the same building at the same time. Even very large charities benefit from occasions in which all their staff can come together. For some it might only be feasible once a year, but it is an ideal way of celebrating success and keeping everyone involved and motivated.

While monthly meetings are important, they are not stand-alone activities. They should be supported by such things as a staff newsletter, noticeboards or websites, the last two for posting general information which needs to be written down and shared, but does not need to go into the newsletter. Noticeboards can also be a good measure of staff morale. An active notice-board with signs of inter-staff measures and up-to-date information indicates a healthy culture, whereas one on which all notices are two years out of date and curling at the edges speaks volumes about how the staff are feeling.

Staff involvement

All internal customers need a forum for feeding back. Team briefings and management meetings are one formal route, while newsletters are more informal but still quite structured. An internal customer care policy will only work if those customers feel valued and listened to; that means actively seeking their suggestions and acting upon them. Quality Circles or a variation of them are one way. Here a voluntary group of staff meet to discuss and suggest solutions for work-related problems. Open staff forums or suggestion schemes are other routes to staff involvement. Bringing together mixed teams of paid staff and volunteers can be a useful way of sharing skills and ideas. It also allows volunteers to feel more involved and ensures that staff teams do not generate a 'them and us' culture towards the voluntary workers.

If you adopt one or all of these measures you will be taking positive steps to creating an organisational culture which listens to and respects its staff (in all their guises), which hears what they say and acts upon it and in which people are valued for their contribution and ideas. That culture will be one in which customers can come first because your staff are confident, motivated and effective.

MONEY, TIME, ENERGY – THERE ISN'T ENOUGH LEFT OVER FOR CUSTOMER CARE

The pressure on the voluntary sector to perform well on limited budgets is, if anything, more intense now than ever before. More charities are competing for the same limited funds; more people are in need of the help they provide, and increasingly the voluntary sector is plugging the gap left by failure of government and statutory authorities to provide the support and services people need. Therefore, for many, the prospect of trying to implement a new policy that doesn't contribute directly to the core mission may seem daunting. However, it needn't use up valuable cash resources and it could save you time and energy in the long run.

An unexpected crisis

A well-established charity working in the area of overseas development started a new fundraising campaign to support projects in Africa. It launched with a series of harrowing newspaper advertisements (paid for by a large corporate sponsor), supported by a piece on local radio and it timed the campaign to coincide with the opening of its new UK headquarters by a Soap Opera celebrity. The public response was amazing, the telephones never stopped ringing and the cheques flooded in. The problem was that it had underestimated the level of interest and it didn't have the people to cope with the donations or the telephone calls. The switchboard was jammed, people couldn't get through and the local radio station got calls of complaint from frustrated donors. To cap it all, one of the relief staff brought in to help became so stressed that she shouted at a caller, who just happened to be the corporate sponsor who had paid for the advertisements.

Firefighting

ARE YOU 'FIREFIGHTING'?

Many organisations handle pressure by reactive crisis management: they 'firefight' and the moment one blaze has been drenched, one problem solved, another springs up and has to be dealt with. Planning, strategy, and good time management all disappear, stress levels increase and productivity suffers – not to mention what happens to any poor customer who might happen to telephone just as you have dealt with crisis number four this morning and it's only 9.30 am!

If you intend to create a customer care culture you have to get out of the 'firefighting' rut. Planning and objectivity are vital, supported by improved time management. This section offers a three-step programme for dealing with a crisis ridden organisation, and a time management checklist to ensure that you have room for customer care.

AVOID THE CRISIS – A THREE-STEP PROGRAMME FOR 'FIRE' PREVENTION

Step One: Investment

Taking a whole day out of the organisation to think about operations, strategy and service delivery often seems an unaffordable luxury – not to mention the anxiety of returning the next day to deal with all the accumulated work that built up while you were away. Many organisations try, therefore, to do all their planning and strategy work after hours or at the weekend – *Don't do this.* A working day spent planning and thinking strategically about how to structure the work, people's time, job allocation and all the other essential operational issues, is a major investment in helping you prevent crises occurring.

Awaydays

Get a facilitator and go to a neutral venue to thrash through issues that you just cannot deal with on a day-to-day basis. Decide on key priorities, commit to taking actions and then return and do them.

Building and maintaining effective communication

Step Two: Clarity and communication

Ensure that everyone knows where their responsibilities start and end. This is not meant to be prescriptive and prevent people from taking an active role in the organisation. But so often 'firefighting' happens because problems get handed around, half-dealt-with by three or four people before being sorted out. This duplication of time and effort is very common, wasting time and creating stress.

Saying no

Learning to say 'No – I will hand this on to Charles when he comes in at 2pm' can be hard. Our instinct is to rush in and sort it out. But if Charles *can* deal with the problem, your involvement merely adds another layer to the confusion, and increases the time spent talking through the issue.

Decide at your awayday who is responsible for what, how you will cover for each others' absences in the event of a crisis and where the buck stops.

Keeping customers informed

If you need to answer the customer, do so in a way that is clear and concise, and reassures them that as soon as the correct person is free to sort out the problem they will do so. Customers do not always expect instant solutions, but they appreciate clarity and communication while they are waiting.

A communication checklist

Listen, Listen, Listen: that means hearing what is said and what is unsaid, reading the non-verbal messages – paying special attention to tone and body language.

Communicate clearly: give people straight messages, avoid euphemisms, abbreviations, acronyms. Don't assume that your customers know the jargon.

Avoid mixed messages: if you mean 'no', say no: don't try to hide behind warm words or your customers will interpret your message as 'yes'.

Stick to the point: don't use twenty words where ten will do. Be precise in what you say and what you mean. Use the KISS principle – Keep It Short & Simple.

Avoid preconceptions: don't jump to conclusions about customers, based on what they look like or sound like – appearances are misleading and judging by stereotypes leads to trouble.

Set deadlines: if you are responding to a complaint or query then give a definite deadline for when you intend to return with an answer, and then stick to it.

Encourage feedback: especially from internal customers. You do not have a monopoly on ideas, so make sure you seek them from those around you.

Shut up: remarkably often a communication goes wrong by virtue of its length, so say your piece and then stop.

Step Three: Proactive not reactive

Provided that your planning and communication systems are in place, then developing a proactive problem-solving culture should be easy. This means spotting the icebergs before you hit them and knowing how to deal with issues before they develop into full-blown crises. Of course, it is not infallible but if you can manage to implement some of the suggestions in this section then 'firefighting' should take up a lot less of your staff's valuable time and energy.

Using time management to save time

Time management is almost as clichéd as TQM, but behind every cliché is a truth worth noting. Good time management is basically about planning, having a sense of what might be coming up ahead and using resources such as people, time, and money for maximum impact. The most obvious thing to say about managing your time is that you will never manage all of it, so allow for the unexpected and interruptions and then you won't feel you have wasted time on them. Try to develop sound time management techniques in your team and with colleagues so that when a crisis occurs you will all be ready for it, and will have the spare capacity to deal with it immediately.

Time Management Technique 1: Be prepared

- Allocate time for each regular team/office task. Make that time untouchable so that key routine tasks get done and the whole place doesn't fall about your ears when you are having to cope with the unexpected.

- Ensure that everyone is kept up to date with key management information so that no time is wasted in repeating details to people who should already know them.

- Delegate routine activities to staff and volunteers, making good use of their time and skills

- Set aside regular slots of time for management/team meetings and consultation time, so that staff know they can tackle managers at a set time to get problems sorted, thereby avoiding constant interruptions and wasted staff time in coming back two or three times to talk to someone who is on the telephone.

- Train your team in customer care and all its techniques. This encourages 'buy in' to the idea and makes sure that you equip individuals to deal effectively and confidently with customers, so they do not pass responsibility back to you all the time.

Time Management Technique 2: Using time efficiently

- Keep meetings short and to a minimum – having a clear agenda with time allocated for each item. Appoint an efficient minute taker to note action points.

- Plan telephone calls – having made a note of the key points before you ring.

- Use staff time effectively by allocating mail opening to one person, answering routine enquiries to another, etc.

- Make sure staff take down all the relevant details when receiving customer calls, have a form if necessary so you know exactly who to call back and about what.

- Develop an awareness of the difference between urgent and non-urgent tasks – giving priority to those which are both urgent and important as opposed to the urgent and unimportant ones.

- Build in windows of unallocated time every day for handling unexpected issues and difficulties. A crisis often starts out as a small problem and only grows because no one has time to deal with it.

- Make time for customers – however inconvenient it feels at the time. See customer time as an investment, not a burden.

Time Management Technique 3: Planning

The secret of successful planning is to allocate dedicated time and resources to a project, giving it a timescale with deadlines for each stage, checking progress at certain points, making sure resources are available before you start, and using the process of planning to highlight where problems may occur. When dealing with customers, planning is often impossible because they are unpredictable in their requests. However anticipating possible requirements can save you time and stress. Having standard forms for enquiries, complaints, suggestions, and feedback means that you always have a mechanism for collecting information and passing it on. By using some of the communication techniques outlined earlier in this chapter both for internal and external customers, you can forewarn people of changes coming up (such as change in location, products, staff, etc) and thereby prevent problems. You can also invite suggestions for improving the implementation of any plans you may have.

Don't keep your plans secret. Share them with staff, volunteers, and external users; encourage feedback and ideas, make the process part of your involvement strategy so that all customers feel they can contribute. Planning frequently fails because people do not start early enough. Everything always takes much longer than you think so, when drawing up a timescale for your plan, allow more time than you think you will need. This means you can still deliver on time without creating extra stress and, if you finish ahead of schedule, you will have created some spare time – what a bonus.

A good planner is someone who is prepared to revise the schedule, adapt the plan to take account of ideas or changed circumstances, and is still able to deliver the goods or services at the planned time and to budget.

IDENTIFYING CUSTOMER TYPES

Technical crews in theatres often say that the production would be superb if it wasn't for the actors getting in the way; so it is with customer care. You need customers – they are an essential part of the process – but sometimes it all goes wrong because of them. Identifying the types of customers you have can help you to get over this problem. We have already done a simple external/internal, direct/indirect analysis, but, if you look in more depth, some distinct characteristics occur which run across these categories. Spotting the customer type can help you match your response accordingly.

Information seekers

This customer is easy to spot. They are the browsers, the gatherer of leaflets and information, those who like to spend time doing their research, exploring every possible angle and scenario before making a decision. On the telephone or in person you can be sure to receive an intensive grilling about the ins and outs of your service, about every aspect of service delivery or product specification. This customer may be making a direct comparison between you and another provider, and will be won round by attentive and sensitive handling. On no account give the appearance of being too busy to deal with them, or thinking their questions are too bizarre or finicky to be answered. Information Seekers do not always turn into customers, but, if you dismiss them as time wasters, they tend to have loud and powerful voices when it comes to criticising the organisation. They are natural complainers and think nothing of telling everyone they know how poor they found your service to be.

Something for nothing

These are the serial complainers of the customer world. They seem to enter any encounter with a ready-prepared complaint and take delight in seeing just how much they can get away with for nothing. It is a sad fact of life that they do exist and all organisations and businesses encounter them. The best way to handle these types is to negotiate a deal in which they do get a discount, or some form of freebie, but not everything they are asking for. The serial complainer is not a big spender, but they make their presence felt, so it is important to try to win them round at the point of contact. But, even if they feel satisfied on the day, it doesn't mean they will not complain again in the future – they can't help it!

Relationship builders

This type of customer wants to work with you. Partnerships and networks matter to them and they are only really happy when they feel involved with the organisation. A simple transaction of money paid for service rendered is not enough – they like to know what makes the organisation tick. They ask questions, refer to staff by name, and remember details about your service that even you might have forgotten. They make good customers because they are loyal and positive about you, so respond to their needs for communication by keeping them well informed, remembering their name, and asking for their input. This is not being patronising – it is seeing a useful source of customer feedback and benefiting from it. Relationship builders can be big external customers as well as small internal ones, so watch out for the signs and meet them more than half way for a rewarding and satisfying partnership.

Users

Some might call these the perfect customer, someone who wants to be given good service, pays for it promptly, walks away happy, and then returns to use your service again when the need arises. A straightforward customer/supplier exchange which doesn't develop beyond that is useful. You need a core of these customers, but not to the exclusion of all others; because they do not want to get involved they are not the people to ask for feedback or suggestions. They do not welcome that degree of intimacy, so don't thrust it upon them.

CHAPTER FIVE

Handling complaints, finding solutions

What is in this chapter?
- types of customer complaints and responses
- listening, negotiation and assertiveness skills
- the importance of body language in handling complaints
- difficult customers – a role play exercise
- handling complaints effectively – guidelines for a complaints procedure
- the seven deadly sins of customer care

EVEN THE NICEST CUSTOMERS COMPLAIN

Customer complaints are a fact of life. However hard you try there will be occasions when the serial complainer walks into your organisation and attempts to do what they do best which is to make your life a misery. Don't worry... this chapter gives you a series of techniques and skills for handling complaints, as well as tips on turning the negatives into positives and, by doing so, converting a critic into a friend.

> **Remember:** happy customers come back and may tell their friends. Unhappy customers never come back and tell at least ten other people of their experience.

COMPLAINTS, COMPLAINTS, COMPLAINTS

What type of complaints or problems are there? Every organisation will have its own horror stories of the type of difficult customer or awkward situation they have had to deal with, but as a rough guide complaints fall into three levels of seriousness, each needing a different response.

Level One: Mild irritation

This sort of complaint arises from a variety of irritating but not life-threatening situations such as having not had telephone calls returned, being kept waiting for a product or service, being passed on from one person to another and having to explain all over again. All these events lead to customers feeling put out, unfriendly towards the organisation and wanting to 'get things off their chest', so they snap at the poor person on the telephone or at the front desk.

Once the person has 'had a go' or made their complaint they nearly always calm down immediately, perhaps feeling embarrassed at having made a fuss, and are more than happy to accept your explanation or solution.

Level One complaints require immediate, but not overblown, response. A simple statement of apology, an acknowledgement of the person's complaint or feelings and an invitation to discuss the solution should do the trick. Something along the lines of: 'I am sorry that you were kept waiting for a response. I can appreciate how irritating that must have been and I apologise for our delay in getting back to you. However, now I am here, how can I help sort the situation out for you?'

CUSTOMER CARE LAW 10: Customers are always right even when they are wrong – so apologise straight away

By apologising you clear the ground for positive action. In cases of mild irritation such apologies should take account of how the person is feeling (read those non-verbal signals carefully) and why. You can defuse any anger that might be building up by apologising and acknowledging why the customer feels as they do; then you are free to move straight on to a solution.

By involving the complainant in seeking a solution, asking for their suggestions or feedback, you swiftly move the situation forward from complaint to resolution. This means that the customer is less likely to keep going over the same ground and more likely to accept your suggestion because their complaint has been heard, and acted upon.

Level One complaints can often be handled by front-line staff, especially if they are secure in the knowledge that their line manager is there to step in and support them if necessary. Allowing the staff who have been on the receiving end to deal with the situation themselves is both empowering for them and more likely to lead to a solution because the response is immediate.

CUSTOMER CARE LAW 11: Always thank the customer even though they have complained

The All Night Party and the Lone Night Porter Story

Recently my mother, husband and our small baby went to a friend's wedding reception in Bristol. We booked into a hotel recommended by the venue hosting the reception and turned up at 10pm to hear a noisy disco in progress. On checking in we asked how long it was likely to go on and were told that it was a private party and would stop at 11pm. By midnight, in our second floor room, we could still hear every word of the songs being played in the basement, so my husband went down to complain. Eventually, following a protracted discussion (in which the night porter admitted he had regular complaints of this kind and sometimes was physically threatened by guests) and a call to the police and environmental health officer, the porter got the music turned down. On the following morning we agreed amongst ourselves that we would only pay 50% of our hotel bill (two rooms). However on checking out, the receptionist's response to our mild mannered suggestion that we might negotiate about the bill was 'I can't do anything about it. I told you it was a private party, I am not authorised to give you a discount'. My reply was 'well, in that case, I am not going to pay anything. You can get your manager to contact me on her return'. Unfortunately for the receptionist, three other guests standing in reception, who had also been disturbed, promptly refused to pay their bills as well, so the hotel lost not only the money for our two rooms but for their three as well.

CUSTOMER CARE LAW 12: Empower your front-line teams to negotiate. They may save the day for you and prevent complaints becoming too serious

Level Two: Serious dissatisfaction, but open to negotiation

By definition these are more serious complaints, often the result of problems built up over time or of serious misjudgements somewhere in the organisation. Although the cause may be beyond our control we have to take responsibility for solving the problem. Some common causes of Level Two complaints are: people being written to time and again for money, when they have said they do not want to donate; letters going unacknowledged; queries being handed around the office; late or wrong products arriving; changes in staff delivering a service resulting in users feeling uncertain and unsupported.

In these situations the customer is already angry by the time the complaint is made. They may be shouting or seething with anger and their immoderate tone is made worse by immoderate language, although not abusive certainly unfriendly. However the tell-tale sign that they are open to negotiation is the use of expressions such as 'and I want to know what you are going to do about it' or 'I want to see the manager'. This is your signal to step in and negotiate. Do not assume that the situation is irrecoverable but you must act quickly and take charge.

Start by apologising and acknowledging their anger 'I am sorry, I can see that you are angry and clearly we have a problem, how can I help?' or 'I see that this has annoyed you, I am sorry about that. Perhaps I can help sort things out'.

If you have just joined the discussion you need to establish the facts. Try to encourage the customer to tell you exactly what the matter is. This is important for two reasons: firstly, you need to hear from them what the issue is and get their words into your head so that you can start work on a solution, and, secondly, by asking them to talk, you create a moment of breathing space for yourself. Use phrases such as 'Would you mind just telling me exactly what the problem is? I know you have explained to my colleague but I need to get the facts direct from you' or 'Could you spare a few minutes to just go over the main problems with me? I'd be grateful, and it would help me to sort things out'.

If at all possible move that person to a neutral area, or, if it is a telephone complaint, ensure you are in a space that is reasonably quiet where you can try to listen carefully. You need to be able to concentrate fully on what is being said to you with no distractions – visual or verbal.

Once they have agreed to tell you what the problem is, listen carefully; clarify as you go along any points that seem vague; try not to be combative or defensive of staff. This is a listening brief to help them get it out of their system and to give you clues as to how to solve the problem. It can be helpful to repeat back what they have said, just taking the salient points, devoid of any emotion or accusation, so that you are both clear about where the difficulties lie.

Once you are clear about the issue, seek suggestions from them about ways forward, along the lines of 'I see now where the problems are. Before I make some suggestions about what we can do, is there anything specific that has occurred to you?' or 'Before I suggest some ways forward, have you any suggestions to help us resolve this?'

Now you negotiate (see later in this chapter on negotiation skills), remembering to deal with each point separately, not to over-commit yourself and to work for Win:Win, the result where both parties emerge with gains.

Once you have reached an agreed solution, then thank the customer for bringing the matter to your attention and close the conversation with a repetition of what action you will take.

The angry man and the large dog

A receptionist working for an animal welfare charity was surprised by a man storming into the front office, swearing and abusing her and all her colleagues because he had been refused permission by the charity to adopt a large dog (he lived in a small town flat). She felt powerless to stop his anger and was quite shaken by the end. Nothing she said would calm him down and he eventually left threatening to return the following day to see her boss.

The receptionist went to her supervisor who immediately offered to contact the customer and explain the policy again, and to be on hand when he next came in. He also suggested that the receptionist call him herself and make an appointment for him to come in again in a couple of days time when the supervisor would be on hand to offer support and prevent the situation getting nasty.

When the man did return he was obviously embarrassed by what had happened and, once the situation had been fully explained again, he accepted a small dog without complaint.

Level Three: All-out fury – call the UN!

Hopefully these will be very few and far between, particularly if you have a proactive customer care culture and well trained staff who can spot a complaint brewing at 100 metres and step in to deal with it. But the general public can be irrational; these events happen but, providing you have a strategy for dealing with them and you have trained your staff in basic negotiation and assertiveness techniques, you should be able to deal with the fallout even if you cannot solve the problem.

Your first step is containment. It is vital that the complainant is removed from public show, out of reception, and if necessary away from the staff member at whom the tirade is directed. Stepping in as the manager, you can help to shift the power balance away from the angry customer back to you.

Let them get rid of their anger, but don't be bullied. There is no need for raised voices and abuse, whatever the source of the complaint and however cross the person is. Try some defusing phrases such as 'I appreciate that you are very angry and I want to hear the reasons why, but please stop swearing and shouting at me. It is not helping' or 'Please stop shouting. I am perfectly willing to hear everything you have to say and I understand how upset you are, but yelling at me is not the answer'.

CUSTOMER CARE LAW 13: Customers have the right to be angry; they do not have the right to be rude or violent

If you suspect that the individual may be violent, have someone with you to make sure things do not get nasty and ensure that you are not locked together in a small room out of sight. Try to get the person to calm down either by having them leave or leaving them alone to get control of their feelings. If necessary having someone standing by in the shape of your security staff or your strongest toughest staff member to help you out if the very worst happens. Take time out to help defuse the situation. Offer them a glass of water or a cup of tea to help calm them down and then go through the situation step by step, taking breaks as necessary for everyone to collect themselves.

It is possible you will not manage to solve this kind of complaint. Sometimes they are beyond solution, so your aim should be to defuse and calm, followed by an agreement in which you agree to disagree and finish with an apology. You want to prevent the customer leaving the organisation intent on saying bad things about you to everyone they meet.

Watchpoint: never get angry with an angry customer. Behaviour breeds behaviour and if you start shouting back then the whole situation will get out of hand.

Whatever type of complaint you face, by acquiring some of the essential skills described below you will be better equipped to deal with all types of difficult customer.

NEGOTIATION

An ability to negotiate successfully is the most useful skill for handling and resolving complaints or difficulties. Of course practice in negotiations improves performance but there is much one can achieve just by following the guidelines given below and then by trying out the role play with colleagues and then thinking up some of your own.

Remember the purpose of any negotiation to reach a Win:Win solution: this means that both sides leave the encounter with a sense of having gained something, without having to surrender all their bargaining points and without feeling bullied or bludgeoned into an agreement. Although compromise has now taken on a pejorative meaning in many peoples' minds implying defeat and surrender, a Win:Win is a compromise in the true sense of the word, a mutual agreement between parties.

A 12-point guide to negotiation

1. Listen actively.
Show that you are not just hearing what they say but that you are really able to understand both the words and the emotions. By doing this you will win over the other party by emphasising that you are able to assess what the key problem is and on what you need to focus your negotiation. Sometimes the real complaint is buried under a pile of irrelevant niggles.

2. Allow the other person time to express their feelings and concerns.
By giving the customer plenty of time, without interruptions, to say their piece you are helping them let off steam, if necessary. It is crucial to have all the issues raised at the beginning, so that you know exactly what you are dealing with.

3. Deal with each point logically; start with the easiest, least contentious issue.
Being able to reach agreement on a simple issue helps create a positive atmosphere in which to tackle the more difficult problems.

4. Summarise any agreements reached as you go.
This is a useful re-enforcing activity which also ensures you make progress instead of revisiting points again and again.

5. Stick to the facts.
Avoid opinions and emotional outbursts. However irrational or emotional the customer is being you must stay calm and focused on the matter under discussion.

6. Give reasons not excuses.
Excuses are no help when dealing with customer complaints. A sensible reason offered without defensiveness is all you need.

The art of active listening
Active listeners use the following techniques:

Playing back – not repeating words verbatim but paraphrasing what has been said to show that you have understood it.

Decoding – by translating the non-verbal messages given by tone or body language, you can show you have understood someone's feelings as well as the meaning in what they have said.

Summarising – picking out the core of what has been said and summarising the essential message so that several ideas may be linked together.

Empathising – putting yourself in the other person's shoes and demonstrating a shared sense of understanding.

7. Defend you staff but don't be defensive.

Do not go for defensive attack, ie, the Tigress defending her young – claws and teeth flashing but no reason. However, never land staff in it (even if they were to blame). Remember the golden rule: 'Praise in public, Criticise in private'.

8. Refer back to their points and seek suggestions as you go.

Include the customer in generating the solution – they are more likely to accept it and it takes the pressure off you.

9. Don't be afraid of taking time out if needed.

Most customer complaints can be dealt with on the spot. If you need to take time out to consult or check details, do so, but remember to explain to the customer what you are doing and why.

10. Use positive language and non-verbal communication.

Open and inclusive gestures and language lower the tension levels of any negotiation (see below in this chapter for suggestions).

11. Try to find a neutral, quiet space for the discussion.

Don't conduct a negotiation in reception on full public view, or by telephone in a crowded office where everyone can eavesdrop.

12. Work for Win:Win.

Remember, it is a mutual solution you are looking for – not victory over the customer, nor complete capitulation on your part.

A customer care role play

You will need to choose two members of your team, one, who is customer focused, to play Role A, and one, who may be less convinced or possibly even hostile to the idea of customer care, to play Role B, plus a team of observers.

Remember that the purpose of role play is to imagine yourself in the situation and try to be as realistic as possible. After the role play is finished observers give feedback on what they saw about body language, communication style, the resolution and what could have been done differently.

Give each role player their individual brief, not letting them see the other person's instructions. Observers are asked not to make personal comments or to criticise acting styles – this is a management exercise, not an audition for drama school!

Role Play: A Grand Day Out

Brief for Role A

You are the director of Open Doors, a charity which provides social activities and day centre services for elderly people in an inner city area. Among the events you organise during the spring and summer are outings such as a day at the seaside, visits to National Trust parks, special open days at places of interest, etc. These events last all day and you provide transport, helpers and a picnic lunch for everyone. Until now the events have been free because they were subsidised by the local authority, but they are cutting their grant and although you have some business sponsorship you think you are probably going to have to charge everyone £2.50 a trip in future (about a fifth of the actual cost). You hadn't intended to tell anyone about this yet, hoping you might be able to persuade the council to change their mind; however it has now leaked out.

Today's trip has not been very successful: the historic house you visited was half shut for emergency repairs, the gardens were partly closed off in preparation for an annual fête and when the picnic lunches ran out, your staff had to rush around trying to get extra food. Two of your more vociferous regular users have just confronted you with a complaint.

Brief for Role B

You are 74 years old and have been a regular user of Open Doors community centre and services for four years now. They provide a day centre and every couple of months during the spring and summer they run bus trips to places of interest such as the seaside or National Trust gardens. The trips are subsidised by the local council and do not cost you anything, and are usually very good. However on the last couple of occasions the staff accompanying the trip haven't been particularly helpful and today's trip was really disorganised. The House was half closed for repairs and the garden looked like a bomb site because of preparations for a big fête due to be held at the week-end. A number of your elderly chums had to make do with crisps and chocolate because the picnics ran out and you have just overheard one of the helpers say that from next month you are all to be charged £5 a head for these outings. As you get off the bus you see the director of the charity and decide to make your feelings known.

Some suggestions as to what you can say if you are taking Role A

I can see how upset you are and I am very sorry that the trip today has been such a disappointment. We are very cross with the National Trust for not warning us about the house closures and we have contacted them asking for a refund so that we can provide an extra trip for everyone as compensation.

As to the lunches, yes, that was a mistake on our part, and all I can do is apologise and do my very best to ensure that it never happens again.

Please do calm down a moment. I know that you and all your friends are concerned about the cost of trips – if I could just be allowed to explain what is happening.

Firstly, the price is not £5, at the very most we will have to charge £2.50 per trip. I know that sounds a lot but if you would let me explain why it is happening and what we at Open Doors are planning to do about it, perhaps that will allay your fears a little.

So far we have not had formal confirmation from the Council that they will be cutting our budget to such an extent that we have to charge. I am still negotiating with the Council at the moment, and I hope to be able to persuade them to change their minds.

However, if they do cut our budget, this is our strategy. To introduce a small charge, for day trips only, of about £2.50 (which is about a fifth of what it costs) for a trial period of six months. During that time we will be actively fundraising from local businesses, and in the local community, and we will need your help here. We want to launch an appeal, and hope that many of you will be involved, perhaps agreeing to do some sponsored events such as card games or dominoes matches. We will be approaching the local radio station for their help and we are planning a big campaign to raise enough money to let Open Doors go on offering its service to as many people as possible for as low a cost as we can.

Now you know the situation, can I count on your support to get others involved?

ASSERTIVENESS
Handling customer complaints assertively

The golden rule when dealing with difficult customers, particularly those who become angry and abusive, is to keep your temper. This can often seem impossible, but by using some basic assertiveness techniques you can regain control of the situation and reach a Win:Win solution.

What is assertive behaviour?

Assertiveness is not aggression; it is not shouting louder, bullying, or seeking to dominate someone else; nor is it about having your own way at all costs. A truly assertive person is an empowering person, someone who allows other people to express their opinions and to show emotions; it is someone who seeks resolutions to conflict and who is prepared to compromise within negotiations to reach agreement. By handling aggressive customers assertively you will be able to calm them down, reduce their aggression and help them to accept your suggestions.

How to negotiate assertively

Listen actively

Use the Active Listening technique outlined earlier in this chapter and don't prejudge the situation. Reinforce your listening with strong non-verbal signals such as nodding your head, having good eye contact and noting down any important points. Avoid writing down every word; this will make the customer feel uncomfortable and will mean that you don't actually listen.

Put your side of the case

Once the customer has finished you must put your side of the case. It is vital that you use assertive language and stick to the facts. You must show assertive behaviour by remaining calm and collected, keeping your feelings well under control. Don't let negative body language betray you.

State what the options are

Here you are on strong positive ground. Offer a range of solutions, outlining the consequences. Giving the customer choices always helps, but be wary of saying too much. Again, stick to facts and concrete offers; avoid woolly promises you can not keep.

Don't be bullied or side-tracked

Do not allow the conversation to get side-tracked by discussing irrelevant issues or by going over and over the same ground. Keep to the point, and do not allow the customer to be bully you by swearing or shouting. If things get heated or you feel you are just getting deadlocked, take the initiative to stop, allowing you both to calm down.

Outline the next steps

Make quite clear to the customer what will or could happen next, both in

---

Assertive language – some examples of words and phrases

- I understand what you are saying, but I do not agree.
- I am sorry you feel that way: How can I help?
- If you would like to explain, I am sure I can sort this out.
- Let's discuss this...
- How can we solve this problem?
- How can we work together on this?
- Why? (questions are an important tool for breaking deadlock or regaining the initiative.)
- No, that just isn't possible, but what I can do is...
- Please do not shout at me.
- So now we have agreed this can we move on to the next point?
- Can we agree on...
- I can see your point, perhaps the best solution would be...
- I think we need to discuss this further...

terms of what you will do and what you expect from them. Again stick to the facts and main points – don't be side-tracked.

Work towards a shared agreement

The most important goal of assertive communication is to reach a mutual agreement: the Win:Win situation that suits you both, where both sides feel happy about the outcome and feel that some of their needs have been met. By using assertive language this should be possible.

Assertive communication is about taking responsibility. Using the personal pronoun and making inclusive comments such as 'let's discuss this', etc, all generate a positive unthreatening environment. Some of these phrases may seem neutral but they are very powerful, especially if delivered in a calm but determined voice, and when reinforced by strong non-verbal signals.

WHAT IS NON-VERBAL COMMUNICATION?

Non-verbal communication is exactly what it says: a way of communicating ideas, moods and feelings through all the non-spoken parts of communication – that is tone, volume, body language and physical presence.

The Complaining Customer in the Menswear Department

I went into my local branch of a large department store to look for a jacket to wear for a wedding, and as I went down the escalator I looked across the store and in the menswear department I could see a customer complaining. Even though I had no idea what he was talking about and was too far away to hear his conversation, everything about him suggested complaint: the way he was standing, his proximity to the shop assistant, his gestures and his furious head movements. I have to confess that, in the name of research, I wandered over to eavesdrop. By the time I got there he was demanding to see the store's general manager and things were getting so heated that I beat a hasty retreat.

With regard to the message we receive when talking to someone face to face, only about 7% of what we remember comes from the words themselves; of the remaining 93%, 38% of the message is made up of vocal signals (ie tone, volume, inflection) and 55% comes from visual signals such as hand or facial gestures. Thus you can pick up some fairly important clues about how a customer is feeling from their non-verbal communication. Here are some of the key things to look for and an interpretation of what they mean.

The vocal non-verbal message

This is made up of two main strands, tone and volume. Let's deal with tone first – that is how a person's voice actually sounds, the pitch and modulation of their voice, and whether it is high or low. When women get angry or upset their voices often get higher (which is why Margaret Thatcher deliberately learned to lower hers when she became Prime Minister) and they speak much more quickly. But a customer speaking in a monotone can be just as dangerous, all that suppressed anger and frustration being held in just below the surface, like a volcano about to erupt.

When it comes to volume, obvious shouting or raised voices can be easier to deal with – because you can take direct action to calm them down. The quiet but steely determination of a customer who appears to be totally in control can hide a rigid determination to get their own way and, however friendly you are, this type of complainant is harder to convince.

With both these types of communication signals you need to remain calm and collected; stay in control by using assertive language and do not let yourself be drawn into a similar communication style, because it will result in deadlock. Shouting back or allowing your own anger to smoulder will not help.

Of course, if you are dealing with a customer complaint on the telephone, these vocal clues become even more important as you are denied any visual indications of how the customer feels. Vocal signals are reinforced by visual signals. Often when we agree to something on the telephone we nod our head, even though no one can see us – sounds daft, but think back to the last time you gave directions to someone over the telephone: I bet you waved you hands about when discussing left turns, right turns and roundabouts! Whenever you are speaking let your natural gestures reinforce the message, even if you are on the telephone. This will make the vocal message stronger because it will show up in your voice.

The visual non-verbal message

Body language is all the physical gestures that make up that 55% of the communication message. What you do with your hands, your feet, whether you lean forward or back, whether you smile or frown – these send out strong signals to the recipient. Sometimes our voices lie while our bodies speak the truth.

When dealing with customer complaints you have to make sure that your body language matches your verbal message. It is no good saying how sorry you are, with a broad grin on your face, or saying 'That's fine. Take as long as you like' while clearly itching to get away and tapping your foot impatiently.

Some examples of positive and negative body language

Positive signals:

- Smiling – when appropriate, and not all the time.

- Nodding your head, not like a mad dog but as a reinforcement gesture while listening.

- Standing slightly back with your head tilted to one side as you listen.

- Offering your handshake in welcome.

- Moving out from behind an obstacle such as a desk or a counter, to join the customer.

- Making and keeping eye contact – not staring straight into a person's eyes but looking at their face while they speak. Direct eye contact should not last longer than 5 seconds for comfort.

- Open gestures – such as reaching towards someone with your hands open, palms tilted towards them.

- Relaxed posture – no crossed arms or hunched shoulders (relaxed breathing helps this).

- Moving – not swaying or dancing about, but not staying glued to the spot either.

- Keeping your distance – with people we don't know between 2-4 feet is most comfortable, making sure you stand facing them.

- Being on the same level, not raised up behind reception, towering over customers, or sitting while they stand.

Negative signals:

- Frowning, screwing up your eyes.

- Fidgeting, twiddling your hair, jangling keys in your pocket, etc.

- Bunching your hands into fists, or using chopping motions, or banging the desk.

- Standing with your body turned away.

- Standing too close, trying to dominate the physical space.

- Sitting behind a desk with the customer having to stand in front of you.

- Not looking at them or, worse still, staring them out.

An important concept to remember when dealing with complaining customers is that body language works like a mirror. If you send out positive signals your customers are likely to find themselves involuntarily copying those gestures and mirroring your positive message. Try it in the office – it is often hard to stay scowling at a colleague when they smile back, not grinning like a clown, just smiling and relaxing their facial muscles into an open pleasant welcoming expression. It takes more muscles to frown than to smile, so take the lazy way and smile at your customers.

CUSTOMER CARE LAW 14: Never say 'It's not my fault'

Handling complaints effectively – a checklist for action

- Stop and listen – don't rush in with a solution.

- Listen carefully – Listen actively.

- Allow the customer to have their say.

- Make a note of key points and refer to them in subsequent discussion.

- Remember that this is a negotiation not a battle.

- Keep calm, be assertive not defensive.

- Work for Win:Win.

- Never say 'Well, no one else has complained'.

- Deal with small immediate issues straight away.

- Never be sarcastic or rude – treat customers with respect and courtesy at all times.

- Don't be bullied into an answer – if you need to consult then do so.

- Explain what you are doing and why – keep the customer informed.

- Involve the customer in the solution- their suggestions may be useful and it certainly helps to win them over to your view-point.

- Do not assume the worst – the customer may just need to tell you how they feel.

- Always thank them for their custom and for bringing their complaint to your attention.

- Don't leave loose ends – if there is unfinished business, be clear about what will happen next.

- Don't take it personally. Complaints happen, so treat them as useful feedback and learn from them.

SETTING UP A COMPLAINTS PROCEDURE

Chapter Six deals with writing a customer care policy. One essential ingredient should be your complaints procedure and, as we have been dealing with handling complaints, this seemed the right place to discuss your best procedures.

If you manage complaints well they can become a way of converting negative attitudes to positive ones. There is no one more powerful than a critic who has been won over and become an advocate of your service: just think of non-smokers who are reformed smokers; their campaigning zeal tends to be far more vigorous than that of people who have never smoked.

Your complaints procedure should follow some simple steps if it is to be effective. The first is to decide what people most complain about. If you can isolate the main causes of complaints then you may be able to prevent them happening, and if it does happen you will be able to respond and prevent a small niggle developing into a major incident. Once you have identified your most common complaint, ask your front-line team and the staff who deal with customers if they have any suggestions about how to handle it. They have the experience, so use it.

Staff on the receiving end of customer frustrations must be equipped to deal with them. Having a well-designed procedure is an important support tool to add to the skills of assertiveness and negotiation described above.

The second step is that you need a method of recording and passing on complaints. A Complaints Form that a staff member can complete with the customer ensures that all the facts are recorded, that the customer can see some positive action being taken, and that you can pass on information to the right person quickly. Make sure that staff are involved in completing the form. By shifting the burden from customer to staff member you immediately create the impression that complaints are taken seriously, and that you are prepared to spend time sorting it out. Simply asking an already dissatisfied customer to complete a form adds insult to injury and leads the customer to suspect that the form will join a mouldering pile on someone's desk, never to be seen again.

The next step is to explain what will happen to the complaint, fixing a timetable and deciding who will handle the complaint. Giving people a specific date or time by which you will respond is vital; the customer can then go away reassured that they will hear from you again, not needing to chase you for an answer.

An acceptable response time on complaints is seven working days, by which time you should have decided why it happened, what you can do about it, taken the necessary action and responded to the customer. This gives you a realistic breathing space, and it also means that if you are able to reply within the working week, then the customer has had their expectations exceeded. If the complaint is very serious, involving a member of staff, or an accusation of professional misconduct or negligence then a holding response from a senior staff member is vital as an interim measure, ie, a short letter within 24 hours assuring the customer that you are taking action on the matter.

The last step is to have a follow-up procedure. Once a complaint has been dealt with, it may be appropriate to go back to the customer at a later date to see if they are satisfied with the eventual product/service they received. This is not always applicable but if it is appropriate then it is a good way of building long-term customer loyalty and reaching that goal of converting critic to supporter. Don't forget to display your complaints procedure clearly for both staff and customers to see. A suggested format for a procedure is outlined below.

A model complaints procedure

If you have a complaint about our services, our product or our staff please tell us:

1. What is the nature of your complaint? Can it be dealt with immediately or would you like it to be referred to a manager or another member of staff? If you need to refer the complaint please go to Step 2.

2. A member of staff will be happy to take down the details of your complaint. Please tell them everything you think is relevant.

3. Thank you for bringing this matter to our attention. We promise to deal with the matter swiftly and to contact you within seven working days to let you know what action has been taken.

The Marks & Spencer example

I was watching a fly-on-the-wall documentary about the Lakeside shopping complex and they showed M&S staff ripping up clothes that customers had brought back after having worn them once or claiming that they were faulty. It was a rather sensational piece of broadcasting and I was duly incensed and fired off a letter that same evening to the Chairman of M&S, complaining and stating my disgust at this shameful waste. Two days later I received a holding letter from his office saying that my letter had been passed on to the PR team and five days after that I received a two-page detailed response to my complaint outlining M&S policy on recycling etc (written on recycled paper I might add). I was duly impressed both by the content of the letters and by the speed of their response. No doubt I was just one of many complainants and the letters were standard ones, personalised with individual names at the top. Nevertheless I turned from critical consumer to pacified consumer and, sadly for my bank balance, I have not cut up my storecard and continue to shop with them.

CUSTOMER COMPLAINT FORM

Customer Contact Details:

Name

Address

Telephone

Nature of Complaint

When did the incident happen?

Was anyone else involved?

What immediate action has been taken?

Does the customer have any suggestions as to what they would like to happen as a result of the complaint

Staff Contact Details – name, department, date and time

Passed on to:

Ignoring customers

THE SEVEN DEADLY SINS IN CUSTOMER CARE

Sin 1. Taking customers for granted

All our customers are important, irrespective of who they are, or whether or not they have paid. Try to make each one feel special and show them they matter to you, every time you see them.

Sin 2. Ignoring customers

The sin committed in countless shops in high streets everywhere: standing there chatting to fellow staff while customers wait for service. What is more important than your customers? Nothing. So do not ignore them, or assume they will be happy because they are regular users.

Sin 3. Saying 'It's not my fault'

You are on the front-line, you are the organisation – and that means they will complain to you. So even if it isn't your fault, never say so. Try to come up with a positive response.

Sin 4. Failing customer expectations

If you have set yourself up as a customer service organisation then you must deliver. You cannot have 'off' days. Your goal should be not just to meet customer expectations but to exceed them, and that means high quality service all the time for everyone.

Sin 5. Failing to respond positively to a complaint

If someone complains then, however unreasonable their complaint appears, you must respond positively. To dismiss a complaint as trivial or to fail to see the potential for converting a negative into a positive is a great mistake.

Sin 6. Being rude to customers

However difficult they are being, never be sarcastic, never be rude.

Sin 7. Forgetting your internal customers

How can your staff and volunteers do a good job if they are unsupported and taken for granted? Think customer all the time – inside and outside.

Writing a Customer Care Policy

What is in this chapter?
- guidelines and advice for writing a customer care policy
- benchmarking – a useful tool for evaluation

WHY HAVE A CUSTOMER CARE POLICY?

One way of ensuring that you develop a positive customer friendly culture in your organisation is to have a written policy, distributed amongst all staff and volunteers, given to all new staff on joining and shared with user consultative groups and support groups. The more people who know about the policy the more potential champions you have. Feedback from users saying things such as 'How does this relate to your customer care policy?' certainly helps to keep the issue in the forefront of people's minds.

Obviously the language and terminology in your policy will strongly reflect your user group or customer base. Given below is an example of how the policy should be structured, key subject headings, a sample complaints procedure and suggestions for action.

GUIDELINES FOR WRITING A CUSTOMER CARE POLICY

Section One: Mission statement and customer care objectives

In any major policy document you should always start with your 'Mission Statement'. This sets the tone of the document, allows you to refer specific policy-related goals and objectives back to your core mission, and makes it clear to all readers that commitments outlined in the policy are not optional 'bolt on' initiatives but form a central part of your overall strategy.

After the 'mission statement' comes your 'customer care objectives'. You need a separate statement which allows you to set out some general principles for customer care as well as highlighting your overall objectives. The detail of how you hope to reach those objectives should be outlined under the 'Goals' section of the policy.

A sample 'objectives' statement

'We are committed to creating a customer friendly environment for all our users, clients, customers, staff, volunteers and colleagues where all customers are treated with respect. We aim to provide high standards of customer care in all our activities and to strive to exceed our customers' expectations. We aim to work in a culture in which quality and excellence are measures of our success in all our dealings with customers.'

Section Two: Setting customer care goals

Goals are the specific, measurable targets that help you achieve your customer care objectives. They must be clearly defined and measurable so that you can evaluate your progress and have a timed deadline. Some will be short term, others long term or ongoing. Your goals form a strategy framework from which to plan concrete tasks and actions that you implement in the organisation: but that doesn't mean you can produce 'motherhood and apple pie' commitments – worthy but woolly – instead of concrete statements.

Some examples of customer care goals

Objective: Creating a customer friendly environment

Goal – to train all staff in basic customer care and communication skills. **Action by:** *immediate and ongoing.*

Goal – to have a clear statement and set of expectations about customer care as part of new staff induction process. **Action by:** *immediate and ongoing.*

Goal – to redesign reception area to create a more welcoming environment. **Action by:** *end of the year.*

Goal – to set up a user/support group to monitor customer care. **Action by:** *within three months.*

Some of these goals are finite, such as redesigning the reception area. Others are ongoing and require regular monitoring to ensure that they are achieved. When you set goals in your policy you must allocate responsibility to a particular, named member of staff. For example, responsibility for staff training in customer care would fall to the personnel manager or person who holds that brief in your organisation. If the staff member or trustee (it is a good idea to allocate some responsibilities to your board of trustees and to have a customer care champion there) leaves, then make sure that the duty is passed on to the replacement person. Details of how you implement the goals on a day-to-day basis do not belong in the policy – that sort of information is part of your operational plan.

Section Three: Policy statements on standards of performance

As well as having goals which may be revised or added to as part of a policy review process, you need to include some standards of performance concerning broader customer care issues for staff and users alike and to help protect staff in vulnerable situations. These operating standards are not meant to be draconian laws on behaviour, but guidelines drawn up in consultation with staff members who have direct user or customer contacts. If they are seen as too prescriptive and too unrealistic then they will be ignored and will have failed to have achieved their purpose.

This section can include statements on customer relationships, communication issues, staff/customer dynamics, health and safety issues, ethical policies, and any other customer related issue that your particular organisation may have to deal with. Some of the ethical issues, for organisations dealing with children, care provision, etc, will already be covered by other policies or organisational strategy, so it may be sufficient to mention them and refer to other documents.

Sample customer relationships standards

- Staff and volunteers are the organisation's ambassadors and as such should be aware of how they communicate with, and appear to, customers.

- All customers are to be treated with respect.

- Staff are expected to be polite to customers, avoid conflict, not argue with customers or refuse to carry out customer requests that fall within the operating remit of the organisation.

- If staff experience abuse or aggression from customers they are to refer immediately to a line manager or senior staff member for assistance.

- Staff and volunteers are free to negotiate with customers within the guidelines and parameters set out for their individual department (on such issues as refunds, discounts, etc).

- Staff will be appropriately dressed within the office and when on customer visits outside the office.

- Staff are expected to remain professional at all times and do their best to uphold the values and standards of the organisation in all their dealings with customers, users and members of the public.

Section Four: Complaints procedure

See the example outlined in Chapter Five under the heading 'Setting up a complaints procedure'.

Section Five: Evaluation

There is no point in having goals and operational targets if you cannot evaluate their effectiveness. The last section of your policy should include a statement of how you intend to measure your progress, what process is in place for review and redesign, and what, if any, follow-up action is required.

You can measure progress using customer numbers as a criterion, with results published either as a numerical or as a percentage figure.

Typical measures might include:

- number of customers seen

- number of customer requests dealt with

- length of time to deliver product/service

- number of repeat customers

Or you can measure success with regard to complaints, including:

- number of complaints received

- length of time each complaint took to process

You can use any of the customer feedback tools described in Chapter Two to assess your customer care, such as focus groups or questionnaires. These yield both quantitative numerical data, eg. 35% of all customers are satisfied with our service, a further 20% are very satisfied; and qualitative data such as personal comments given on questionnaires or in discussions.

However, in order to measure progress over a period of time it is necessary to set up some benchmarks for standards of performance within the organisation, and if possible against similar sized organisations working in the same field.

BENCHMARKING – A USEFUL TOOL FOR EVALUATION

Benchmarking is a process of identifying areas of best practice either within an organisation, or in another organisation that has similar characteristics in terms of size, personnel, budget and field of expertise. The process allows you to monitor and evaluate specific initiatives or activities against a high quality 'norm' to see whether or not you are reaching or exceeding a level of excellence. This means deciding on a level of excellence in delivering customer care, for example as demonstrated by an individual department, and then trying to replicate that standard across the organisation, consistently and over a period of time.

For example, if you are a national organisation with regional offices, you may find that the office in one part of the country is excellent at responding to user complaints. They respond within two working days and have converted 75% of all complaints into repeat business. This is a best practice benchmark by which you can measure the performance of other offices across the country.

Beware of setting up rivalry between departments or regional teams – benchmarking is not a competitive tool. It is meant to be a facilitating and enabling process which allows the sharing of experience and best practice. If you think, using the example outlined, that 75% is an unrealistic target, then set the benchmark at 50%, which is within the scope of all teams but not unrealistically high.

A benchmarking process needs a period of time to be effective; it cannot happen over night. Allow at least 12 months for the process to gain acceptance and become an operating norm and then collect data every 3 or 6 months and produce an annual analysis of the results.

No one is going to support a process which generates more paperwork unless they can see the organisational benefits, so make sure your benchmarks are relevant to the organisation, easy to define, and challenging enough to generate commitment but not so unrealistic that people feel there is no point in trying to reach them.

AND FINALLY...

There will be times when despite your best efforts, everything seems to conspire against you to frustrate your well laid customer care plans. Don't be too hard on yourself – even the best organisations get it wrong occasionally. I hope the ideas and action plans in this book have illustrated that, with some forethought and planning, and with the enthusiasm of staff, you can create a customer-friendly culture that significantly benefits both your users, customers or clients, and your staff, as well as making yours a more effective organisation.

Customer care *should* be as integral to voluntary sector organisations as fundraising is. It should be part of your strategy and planning process because a close positive relationship with customers is what ensures that charities are providing not just services but solutions to their clients. Internal and external customers matter. Establishing a strong communication link which allows for feedback and suggestions means that you will, by definition, be one step closer to achieving your aims and objectives: not just meeting but exceeding expectations of those you work with and for.

Remember that it takes as much effort to get it wrong as to get it right – so aim high and you will be a success.

APPENDIX 1
The 14 Customer Care Laws

CUSTOMER CARE LAW 1: All customers are equal – regardless of whether they pay for your service or not

CUSTOMER CARE LAW 2: Customer care means not just meeting but exceeding your customers' expectations

CUSTOMER CARE LAW 3: Never make assumptions about your customers

CUSTOMER CARE LAW 4: Listen to your customers

CUSTOMER CARE LAW 5: When you gather customer feedback, do something with it

CUSTOMER CARE LAW 6: Consistency counts in customer care

CUSTOMER CARE LAW 7: Image is based on perception and you cannot control perceptions – only influence them

CUSTOMER CARE LAW 8: Always answer the telephone within 4 rings – you never know who is on the other end of the line

CUSTOMER CARE LAW 9: Your welcome must be professional and friendly while your service is immediate and effective

CUSTOMER CARE LAW 10: Customers are always right even when they are wrong – so apologise straight away

CUSTOMER CARE LAW 11: Always thank the customer even though they have complained

CUSTOMER CARE LAW 12: Empower your front-line teams to negotiate. They may save the day for you and prevent complaints becoming too serious

CUSTOMER CARE LAW 13: Customers have the right to be angry; they do not have the right to be rude or violent

CUSTOMER CARE LAW 14: Never say 'It's not my fault'

APPENDIX 2

Sample questionnaire

This questionnaire has been designed by The Very Good Charity to try to find out what our customers think of our high street shops. Please take a few minutes to complete it and put it in the box by the door. If you would like to add your name and telephone number we will enter you for our prize draw – first prize: £20 voucher to spend on any item in our new Christmas range.

Please tick the box, or comment where appropriate

1. How often do you shop in The Very Good Charity Store? -

❑Once a week   ❑Once a Fortnight   ❑Once every couple of months

❑Very occasionally   ❑This is the first time

2. Overall, what is the thing that attracts you most about The Very Good Charity Store?

❑Range of goods   ❑Helpfulness of staff   ❑Prices

❑Other - please state

3. Would you prefer to see more or less of the following items

	More	Less
Clothes	❑	❑
Books	❑	❑
Toys & Games	❑	❑
Children's clothes	❑	❑
Shoes	❑	❑
Household goods	❑	❑
Gifts	❑	❑
New items such as stationery, gifts	❑	❑
Equipment, tools, etc	❑	❑

4. How would you rate our shop staff on the following points?

	Excellent	Good	OK	Poor
Helpfulness	❑	❑	❑	❑
Knowledge about products	❑	❑	❑	❑
Speed and efficiency	❑	❑	❑	❑
Friendliness	❑	❑	❑	❑

5. What do you like best about shopping in The Very Good Charity Store?

6. What do you like least ?

7. Which other charity shops in the town do you use?

    ❑ Oxfam

    ❑ Cancer Research

    ❑ Help the Aged

    ❑ Scope

    ❑ British Heart Foundation

    ❑ Local charity shop

8. Do you have any comments to make about our service or products? If so please write them here:

Thank you very much for your help.

If you wish to be entered for our prize draw please complete this section.

Name: _____

Telephone: _____

APPENDIX 3

Sample questionnaire

This questionnaire has been designed to assist service organisations, such as those providing home visits or day care help, to assess and monitor the effectiveness of their customer care, even if the customers themselves are non-paying clients or service users. The questions are quite broad but could easily be adapted to fit a range of different customer groups.

Please tick the box, or comment where appropriate

1. How often have you used the service in the past year?

❑ Frequently   ❑ Regularly   ❑ Once or twice only

2. Who suggested /nominated you for this service?

❑ Yourself   ❑ A carer   ❑ Social Services   ❑ Other

3. Do you see the same person each time?   Yes/No

4. Would you prefer to see the same person each time?   Yes/No

5. What are the most important aspects of the service to you?

Please number in order of importance:

❑ Human contact

❑ Having someone to listen to problems / concerns

❑ Having home visits

❑ Knowing someone is available to take up problems on my behalf

❑ The actual help I receive

❑ Continuity of care

❑ Access to a network of services

❑ Other - please list

6. Overall, how would you rate the service you receive?

❏Excellent   ❏Good   ❏Adequate

❏Needs Improving   ❏Poor

7. Do you receive any other similar services, such as meals on wheels, home help, etc? Please list:

If yes, how does our service compare with those?

❏Better   ❏The same   ❏Less good

8. What recommendations or suggestions for changes could you make to help us improve our customer care?

9. Who else do you think we should talk to about our service?

e.g.,

❏ Members of your family who help with your care

❏ Professional carers

❏ Other

Thank you very much for your help.

If you wish to be entered for our prize draw please complete this section.

Name: _____

Telephone: _____

Also available from the DSC...

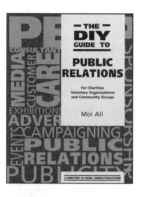

THE DIY GUIDE TO PUBLIC RELATIONS
Moi Ali

A really lively guide to every aspect of PR, from events to publications from media relations to customer care. Written by a consultant with wide experience of working with charities, this updated & expanded edition contains much to stimulate the beginner and refresh the professional. Includes many illustrated examples.
"...practical, logical and easy to use...invaluable." (Third Sector)
246x189mm, 192 pages, 2nd edition, 1999.
ISBN 1 900360 53 5   £12.50

THE DIY GUIDE TO MARKETING
Moi Ali

A dynamic and user-friendly guide to making the very most of your marketing budget. Covers market research, image, identity, branding, advertising, direct mail, and strategy. Packed with tips and case studies, this book will help you take a fresh approach to the way you market your organisation.
244x169mm, 176 pages, 1st edition, 1996.
ISBN 1 873860 97 8 £12.50

THE DIY GUIDE TO CHARITY NEWSLETTERS
Chris Wells

Aimed particularly at those with a limited budget who are trying to keep in touch with donors and supporters, this stimulating book covers starting a newsletter, editing, design, writing skills, and selling advertising space.
"This little gem stands out...because of the clear, accessible writing style and excellent tips." (Voluntary Voice)
246x189mm, 96 pages, 1st edition, 1995.
ISBN 1 873860 11 0 £10.95

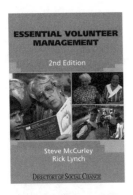

ESSENTIAL VOLUNTEER MANAGEMENT

Steve McCurley & Rick Lynch

With a foreword by Alun Michael MP, Minister of State, Home Office

This number one bestselling book on volunteer management has been revised and updated for UK readers. Lively and user-friendly, it is packed from cover to cover with expert advice. Its contents include: planning for a volunteer programme, creating motivating volunteer jobs, recruitment, screening and interviewing, orientation and training, supervision, retention and recognition, and volunteer/staff relations. 244x169mm, 216 pages, 2nd edition, 1998. ISBN 1 900360 18 7 £14.95

THE HEALTH & SAFETY HANDBOOK

Al Hinde & Charlie Kavanagh *Edited by Jill Barlow*

This step-by-step guide has been specially produced to help and support voluntary and community organisations in conforming to basic health and safety requirements – for employers, volunteers and anyone using your premises. Its contents include: fire prevention and certificate; employers' liability insurance; first aid; incidents and accidents; health, safety and welfare; workplace assessments; and health and safety policy. *"Any organisation wanting to get to grips properly with its health and safety responsibilities, will be rewarded if they purchase this book."* (NACVS) Published in association with Liverpool Occupational Health Project A4, 96 pages, 1st edition, 1998. ISBN 1 900360 25 X £12.50

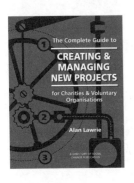

THE COMPLETE GUIDE TO CREATING AND MANAGING NEW PROJECTS

Alan Lawrie *Supported by NatWest*

This practical book looks at how new projects can be developed, tested, designed and established, within or outside existing organisations, how common problems can be tackled and how the work can best be organised, planned and managed. It features case studies, practical guides, checklists and exercises to help with your feasibility planning and will be invaluable to anyone seeking to provide new voluntary sector services, activities or ventures. *"...a motivating and enjoyable read."* (Voluntary Voice) 244x169mm, 136 pages, 1st edition, 1996. ISBN 1 873860 91 9 £12.50

THE COMPLETE GUIDE TO BUSINESS AND STRATEGIC PLANNING

Alan Lawrie *Supported by NatWest*

Business plans and strategic planning, increasingly demanded by funders, can also help your organisation achieve its aims. This practical guide will help you draw up realistic plans and implement them effectively. Don't forget that major Lottery applications also have to be supported by a business plan! *"Crammed with templates to organise your thinking and planning...a winner!"* (BAFM) 246x189mm, 106 pages, 1st edition, 1994. ISBN 1 873860 61 7 £10.95

MANAGING PEOPLE
Gill Taylor & Christine Thornton

This lively book covers the five key areas of people management: supervision, planning and teamwork, dealing with difficult situations, management committee, and letting go. The topics are presented in scenario format, to help bring alive issues, ideas and dilemmas. Each scenario shows how to come to a satisfactory solution and gives action tips and practical advice.
"[An] excellent new book...I wish I had had it when I was starting out as a manager." (Voluntary Voice)
246x189mm, 128 pages, 1st edition, 1995.
ISBN 1 873860 47 1 £10.95

MANAGING QUALITY OF SERVICE
Alan Lawrie

This popular title addresses the ways in which voluntary sector funding contracts now emphasise measurement and accountability, and sheds new light on the potentially fraught process of quality assurance. It shows how intelligent monitoring systems and processes can be beneficial, enable an organisation to gain a sense of achievement, increase internal knowledge of which services and activities deliver sustainable and valued results, and create a feeling of purpose and progress within the organisation.
246x189mm, 104 pages, 1st edition, 1995.
ISBN 1 873860 86 2 £10.95

MANAGING RECRUITMENT AND SELECTION
Gill Taylor

Aims to equip workers and interview panels with the necessary skills and information to make a better job of the recruitment process. Equal opportunities good practice is covered as an integral part of each chapter. Scenarios offer sample situations and offer tips for introducing good practice policies and procedures.
246x189mm, 128 pages, 1st edition, 1996.
ISBN 1 873860 85 4 £10.95

MANAGING ABSENCE
Sarah Hargreaves, Christina Morton, Gill Taylor

Whether voluntary or enforced, staff absence can have a major impact on service delivery. This useful new book will help all trustees and managers of voluntary organisations ensure quality of service whilst maintaining good practice as employers.
Published by Russell House Publishing Ltd
Large format, 128 pages, 1998.
ISBN 1 898924 17 1 £14.95

Coming in 1999...
Managing Conflict
Gill Taylor
ISBN 1 900360 28 4

Index

About the Directory of Social Change

Set up in 1975, the DSC is now one of the largest independent organisations to serve the needs of the voluntary sector. Its aims are to support the voluntary sector by:

- giving voluntary and community groups the information and skills they need to meet their objectives
- encouraging groups to network and share information, thus developing a sustainable future for UK voluntary activity
- campaigning to protect and promote the interests of the sector as a whole.

In addition to researching and publishing reference guides and handbooks we also offer a number of other services.

Courses & Conferences

Tel. 0171 209 4949

We run the largest programme of training courses, seminars and conferences in the UK voluntary sector. Our training courses – like our publications – cover the key skills needed in the sector.

Our conferences and seminars focus on the latest important issues affecting the voluntary sector.

Charityfair

Tel. 0171 209 4949

Charityfair is the biggest annual event for the UK's voluntary sector. Charityfair 98 attracted over 11,000 people to benefit from the most extensive selection of training, advice and debate for charities to be found under one roof.

Charityfair 99 takes place at London's Business Design Centre from Tuesday 20 to Thursday 22 April. Make sure you are on our free mailing list to receive our free events guide, available January 1999.

Charity Centre

Tel. 0171 209 1015

The Charity Centre at Stephenson Way provides five training or meeting rooms, a large conference room and library. Also located at the Charity Centre is London's largest charity bookshop, where the entire range of DSC books and many other titles can be bought over the counter.